STEP INTO THE WORLD OF...

NORTH AMERICAN INDIANS

Michael Stotter

Consultant: Michael Johnson

LORENZ BOOKS

First published in 1999 by Lorenz Books

© Anness Publishing Limited 1999

Lorenz Books is an imprint of
Anness Publishing Inc.,
27 West 20th Street
New York, NY 10011
(800) 354-9657

ISBN 0 7548 0216 7

Publisher: Joanna Lorenz
Managing Editor, Children's Books: Gilly
Cameron Cooper
Editor: Jayne Miller
Project Editor: Joanna Hanks
Designer: Margaret Sadler
Illustration: Rob Ashby, Vanessa Card, Clive Spong,
Shane Watson
Photography: John Freeman
Stylists: Konica Shankar, Melanie Williams
Reader: Penelope Goodare
Production Controller: Ann Childers

Anness Publishing would like to thank Sue Grabham for her
help in creating this book. Anness Publishing would also like
to thank the following children for modeling for this book:
Jamal Ali, Nathanael Arnott-Davies, Hazel Askew, Rhiannon
Atkins, Sarah Bone, Trung Chu Vinh, Rory Clarke, Daniel
Haston, Kane Ives, Eka Karumidze, Bianca Loucaides, Daniel
A. Otalvora, Sarah Louise Phillips, Simon Paul Anthony
Thexton, Shahema Uddowlla-Tafader, Isemfon Udoh.

PICTURE CREDITS

b=bottom, t=top, c=center, l=left, r=right

AKG Photos 2b, 9r, 10l, 12l, 15br, 17tr, 19tc, 19bl, 20bl, 26bl, 27tr, 31tr, 32b, 37l,
41t, 42bl, 43tl, b, 44bl, br, 50tl, 51tr, 56tr, 57t; Corbis-Bettmann 11cl, 13tr, 14cr, 16tl,
18bl, 22c, 24b, 25bl, 27bl, 28bl, 30cl, 33cl, 36br, 38bl, 40tl, b, 41bl, 42br, 45t, cl, 47t,
49tr, 50bl, 51bl, 54b, 60bl, br; Corbis 4, 5br, 10tr, 23tl, c, 17tl, 20br, 20c, 15tr, 26tr,
29c, 33tl, br, 41br, 42tl, 44tr, 54tl, 55tl, c, bl, br, 58bl, 59bl, 60tl, 61tr, c, bc, bl;
CM Dixon Cover tl, back cover tl, tr, br, 2tr, 5tl, 5tc, 5tr, 11tr, cr, 15bl, 17bl, 22l, 22tr,
23bl, 24cl, 29tr, 31tl, 32tr, 33tr, 34l, 35tl, bl, c, tr, 36l, 37tr, 45bl, 46tl, 48tr, c, bl,
51tl, c, 52tl, 53tr, c, bl, 57c, 58tl, r, 59tr, tl; Peter Newark's Pictures Cover bl, 1, 2b,
3r, 8tl, tr, 9tl, tc, 11tl, 12tr, 14l, 15tl, tr, 17tc, 18tr, 19tr, 20tr, 21tl, 23bl, tr, 25c, 27tl,
28tr, br, 29tl, bl, 33bl, 34tr, 36tr, 38tr, 39tl, bl, 43tr, 45br, 46tr, b, 47b, 48bl, 52br,
56br, 59bc.

Printed and bound in Singapore

10 9 8 7 6 5 4 3 2 1

CONTENTS

The First Americans

DESCENDANTS OF THE ANASAZIS, who were among the earliest known North American Indians, have colorful tales of their origins. One story tells how their ancestors climbed into the world through a hole. Another describes how all of the tribes were created from a fierce monster who was ripped apart by a brave coyote. The early history of the many nations or tribes is not clear, though archaeological finds have helped to build a picture of their way of life. If you could step back to before A.D. 1500, you would find that the United States and Canada were home to hundreds of different native tribes. Each had its own leader(s) and a distinctive language and culture. Some tribes were nomadic, some settled permanently in large communities. Remains of pottery, woodcarvings and jewelry show how many of the North American peoples developed expert craft skills.

KEEPING THE PAST ALIVE
Descendants of the different tribes survive throughout North America, passing down stories and traditions to new generations. This boy in Wyoming is dressed in ceremonial costume for a modern powwow. He is helping to preserve his tribe's cultural history.

BRIDGING THE GAP
Archaeological evidence suggests that the first American Indians traveled from Asia. They crossed ice and land bridges formed at the Bering Strait around 13,000 B.C. or earlier. From here, they moved south, some settling along the coasts.

TIMELINE 32,000 B.C.–A.D. 1400

Most historians believe that hunters walked to North America from Siberia. Evidence suggests there may have been two migrations—one around 32,000 B.C., the second between 28,000 B.C. and 13,000 B.C. Some historians think there may have been earlier ancient populations already living there. More research is needed to support this theory. The hunters spread out, each group, or tribe, adapting their way of life to suit their environment. Later, some gave up the nomadic hunting life and began to settle as farmers.

serpent mound of the Hopewell culture

3000 B.C. Inuit of the Arctic are probably the last settlers to come from Asia.

1000 B.C. Early cultures are mound builders such as the Adena and later, the Hopewell people. The Hopewell are named after the farmer on whose Ohio land their main site was found.

1000 B.C. Farming cultures develop in the Southwest with agricultural skills brought from Mexico.

black and yellow corn

300 B.C.–A.D. 1450 Cultures, such as the Hohokam, use shells as currency.

A.D. 200 (or before) There is evidence of corn being grown by the mound-building people, probably introduced from Mexico.

A.D. 700–900 Pueblo people bury their dead with black and white painted Mimbres pots.

burial pot

32,000 B.C.

3000 B.C.

300 B.C.

BUCKSKIN RECORD

Tales of events were painted on animal skins, such as this one, created by an Apache. The skins serve as a form of history book. North American Indians had no real written alphabet, so much of the evidence about their way of life comes from pictures.

FALSE FACE

Dramatic, carved masks were worn by several tribes to ward off evil spirits thought to cause illnesses. This one is from the Iroquois people. It was known as a False Face mask because it shows an imaginary face. False Face ceremonies are still performed in North America today.

DIGGING UP EVIDENCE

Hopewell Indians made this bird from hammered copper. It dates back to around 300 B.C. and was uncovered in a burial mound in Ohio. The mounds were full of intricate trinkets buried alongside the dead. Finds like this tell us about the crafts, materials and customs of the time.

ANCIENT TOWN

Acoma *(right)* is one of the oldest continuously inhabited traditional Pueblo settlements in the Southwest. It is still partly inhabited by Pueblo descendants. The Pueblo people were given their name by Spaniards who arrived in the area in 1540. *Pueblo* is a Spanish word meaning village. It was used to describe the kind of tribe that lived in a cluster of houses built from mud and stone. Flat-roofed homes were built in terraces, two or three stories high.

A.D. 700 Mound-building cultures build temples at Cahokia near the Mississippi River. The city holds the largest population in North America before the 1800s.

A.D. 900 Earliest Anasazis (ancient people) on the Colorado Plateau live in sunken pit homes. Later, they build their homes above the ground but keep pit dwellings as kivas, which are their religious buildings.

kiva (underground temple) of the Anasazis

A.D. 982 First Europeans reach Greenland (northeast of Canada) under the Viking, Erik the Red.

A.D. 1002 Leif Eriksson lands in Newfoundland, Canada, and creates the first European settlements.

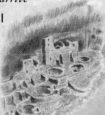

Vikings arrive

A.D. 1100 Anasazi people move into the mountains, building settlements in cliffs.

Mesa Verde, a cliff palace

A.D. 1200 The Calusa in Florida are skillful carvers and craftsmen who trade extensively.

1270s–1300 Anasazis abandon many of their prehistoric sites and stone cities—many move eastward.

1300 Beginnings of the Pueblo tribes (Hopi and Zuni) in the Southwest. Many of these are descendants of the Anasazis.

A.D. 700

A.D. 1400

Inhabiting a Vast Land

THE FIRST NORTH AMERICANS were hunters who followed musk oxen, bison and other animals to the grassland interior of the huge continent. Early settlements grew up in the rugged, hostile terrain of the Southwest where three dominant cultures evolved. The Mogollon (Mountain People) are thought to be the first Southwest dwellers to build houses, make pottery and grow their own food, starting around 300 B.C. The Hohokam (Vanished Ones) devised an extensive canal system to irrigate the desert as early as 100 B.C., while the Anasazi (Ancient Ones) were basket makers who built their homes high among the cliffs and canyons. In contrast, the eastern and midwestern lands abounded with plant and animal life. Here, tribes such as the Adena (1000 B.C. to A.D. 200) and the Hopewell (300 B.C. to A.D. 700), created huge earth mounds to bury their dead. The central Great Plains was home to over 30 different tribes, who lived by hunting bison. In the far north, the Inuit had a similar existence, relying on caribou and seals for their food and clothes. Europeans began to arrive around A.D. 982 with the Vikings. Then, in the 1500s, Spanish explorers came looking for gold, land and slaves. Over the next 400 years, many other foreign powers laid claim to different parts of the land. By 1910, the native population was at its lowest, about 400,000, and many tribes had been forced from their homelands on to reservations.

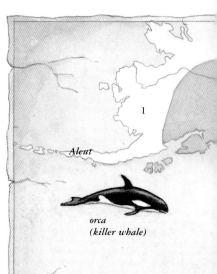

Aleut

orca (killer whale)

TRIBAL HOMELANDS
In the 1400s, there were more than 300 tribes, or nations, spread across North America (between two and three million people). These are often divided into ten cultural areas based on the local environment:
1 Arctic
2 Subarctic
3 Woodlands
4 Southeast
5 Great Plains
6 Southwest
7 Great Basin
8 Plateau
9 Northwest Coast
10 California.

TIMELINE A.D. 1400–1780

1400 Apaches arrive in the Southwest, probably by two routes—one from the Plains after following migrating buffalo, the other via the Rockies.

1492 Christopher Columbus sails from Spain to the Bahamas, where he meets the peaceful, farming Arawaks.

1510 The powerful Calusas of Florida abandon their ancient center, Key Marco, an island made from shells, possibly after hearing of foreign invaders.

1513 Calusas drive off Ponce de León.

Columbus

1541 Zuni people get a first glimpse of horses when Spain's Francisco Vasquez de Coronado travels to the Southwest.

1541 Caddo people of the Plains oppose Spanish Hernando de Soto's soldiers.

1542 The large Arawak population that Columbus first encountered has been reduced to just 200 people. Ten years later the Arawaks die out due to mistreatment.

shell wampum belt celebrates the League of Five Nations

1550 League of Five Nations is formed by the Seneca, Cayuga, Mohawk, Oneida and Onondaga tribes in the northeast to create a strong government. They are referred to as the Iroquois.

1585 Sir Walter Raleigh reaches the northeast coast and, ignoring the rights of the Secotan natives, claims the land for the English, calling it Virginia.

1590 Raleigh and John White return to Virginia, but the colony has disappeared. White draws pictures documenting Secotan life.

1400   1540   1550   1595

BAFFIN
ISLAND

seal

1

2

Hudson Bay

Inuit with igloo

Inuit fisherman

NEWFOUNDLAND

QUEBEC

Tsimshian

9

Cree

Chipewyan canoe

Cree

2

Cree

Plains Cree

Blackfoot   Hidatsa

8   *salmon*

Plains Ojibwa

Mandan

Crow

Nez Perce   Western Sioux

Shoshone   Pawnee

Ojibwa

beaver

Algonquin

Huron

3

New York

Chippewa   Iroquois

Menominee   Algonquian

groups

Washington

Shawnee

Powhatan

Arapaho   *corn*   Sioux

7   Ute

Missouri River

Mississippi River

Salish

Washoe

Cayuse

Yurok

10

*Paiute
basket- maker*

*Cheyenne warrior
hunting bison*

Hopewell mound

Secotan
village

N

*Hopi
kachina
doll*

Osage

Cherokee
village of Echota

eagle

Kiowa camp

Chickasaw   Creek

Choctaw   Seminole

Chumash

Los Angeles • Mohave

*Navajo
hogans*

NEW
MEXICO

5   Wichita

Apache   Comanche

TEXAS

4   Natchez

Calusa   eagle

Miami

6

Pueblo village

1598 Juan de Onate founds the first Spanish colony on Pueblo Indian land.

1600s Shoshone acquire horses from the Southwest (brought there by Spanish invaders), and they spread across the Great Plains.

horses on the Plains

1607 Jamestown colony is founded on Powhatan land.

1607 Pamunkey members of the Powhatan Confederacy take John Smith prisoner.

1620 The Mayflower Pilgrims arrive on the east coast and are helped by the Wampanoag.

1650 Guns from European traders (at first flintlocks, later rifles) begin to take the place of traditional weapons.

1707 A Russian expedition reaches the Northwest Coast to discover that it is inhabited.

willow bow

*coup
stick*

rifle

1722 League of Five Nations increases to six when the Tuscarora join the group.

1774 Juan Perez sails to the Northwest Coast to take the land for Spain. Smallpox, from the Europeans, almost wipes out the Haida people.

Around 1750, Sioux tribes move to the Plains.

1771 Five Franciscan missions are set up on Chumash land in California (this leads to a revolt in 1824).

1620   1710   *Haida totem pole*

7

POCAHONTAS (1595–1617)
The princess became a legend, and the topic of a Disney film, for protecting English Captain John Smith against her father, Chief Powhatan. The English took Pocahontas captive to force Powhatan's people to agree to their demands. She married John Rolfe, an English soldier, and in 1616 left for England with their baby. She never returned, and died of smallpox, in England, at the age of 22.

Brave and Bold

MANY NORTH AMERICAN Indians who have earned a place in history lived around the time that Europeans reached North America. They became famous for their dealings with explorers and with the white settlers who were trying to reorganize the lives of American Indian nations. Some tribes welcomed the new settlers. Others tried to negotiate peacefully for rights to their own land. Those who led their people in battles, against the settlers, became the most legendary. One of these was Geronimo, who led the last defiant group of Chiricahua Apaches in their fight to preserve the tribe's homeland and culture.

CORNPLANTER (died 1796)
In the 1700s, Cornplanter was a chief of the Iroquois Confederacy. He was a friend to the Americans and fought on their side in the Revolution of 1775–83. Seneca lands were spoiled, but Cornplanter's people were given a reservation for their help. Many Iroquois people fought on the side of the British, which split the group.

Opechancanough, Powhatan

Black Hawk, Sauk

Geronimo, Apache

Pontiac, Ottawa

Lapowinsa, Lenape

TIMELINE A.D. 1780–1924

1783 The colonists (settlers) sign a treaty with Britian, which recognizes their independence and calls them Americans. The tribes are never regarded as American.

1788 The Chinook in the Northwest have their first encounter with Europeans when they meet Englishman, John Mears.

1789 Explorers encounter Kutchin and other Subarctic tribes, who later set up trade with the Hudson's Bay Company (formed in 1831).

1795 Tecumseh refuses to sign the Treaty of Greenville giving up Shawnee land.

William Clark and Meriwether Lewis

1803 The United States federal government buys Mississippi land from the French, squeezing out the tribes even more.

1804 Sacawagea guides Lewis and Clark on the first overland journey from Mississippi to the Pacific Coast.

1830–40s Painters such as Frederic Remington, George Catlin and Karl Bodmer, document lifestyles of the Plains Indians.

1832 Sauk chief, Black Hawk, leads a final revolt against the United States and is defeated.

1848 Discovery of gold in California.

1848–58 Palouse tribe of the Plateau resist white domination, refusing to join a reservation.

George Catlin painting a Mandan chief

coming of the train

1780

1803

1848

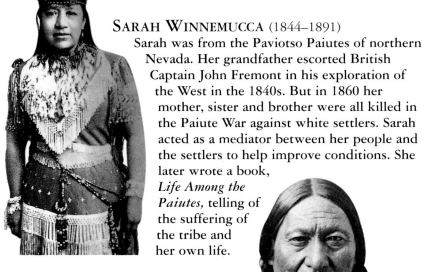

SARAH WINNEMUCCA (1844–1891)

Sarah was from the Paviotso Paiutes of northern Nevada. Her grandfather escorted British Captain John Fremont in his exploration of the West in the 1840s. But in 1860 her mother, sister and brother were all killed in the Paiute War against white settlers. Sarah acted as a mediator between her people and the settlers to help improve conditions. She later wrote a book, *Life Among the Paiutes,* telling of the suffering of the tribe and her own life.

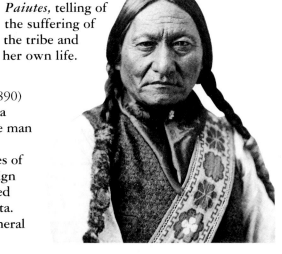

SITTING BULL (1831–1890)

The Hunkpapa Sioux had a spiritual leader, a medicine man known as Sitting Bull. He brought together sub-tribes of the Sioux and refused to sign treaties giving up the sacred Black Hills in South Dakota. He helped to defeat of General Custer at Little Bighorn.

TECUMSEH (Died 1813)

A great chief of the Shawnees, Tecumseh, tried to unite tribes of the Mississippi valley, Northwest and South against the United States. He even fought for the British against the United States in the 1812–14 war. The picture shows his death.

PROTECTING THEIR TRIBES

These eight North American chiefs are some of the most famous. Not all fought. Lapowinsa of Delaware, was cheated out of land when he signed a contract allowing settlers as much land as they could cover in a day and a half. Pontiac traded with the French but despised English intrusion. Chief Joseph tried to negotiate peacefully for land for the Nez Perce tribe but died in exile. Red Cloud successfully fought to stop gold seekers invading Sioux hunting grounds.

Oscelo, Seminole

Red Cloud, Sioux

Chief Joseph

1850s–80s Railways open up the West to settlers.

1850 The Navajo sign their third treaty with the United States, but hostilities continue.

1864 The Long Walk—Navajo people and animals are massacred by United States troops, their homes burned. Survivors are forced to walk 300 mi. to Fort Sumner.

1864 Sand Creek Massacre—300 Cheyenne women and children are killed by United States soldiers.

Sand Creek Massacre

1876 General Custer is killed by Sioux warriors in the Battle of Little Bighorn.

1886 Surrender of Geronimo to the United States. He is a prisoner.

1890 Ghost dance springs up as Sioux tribes mourn their dead—it worries the white settlers who see it as provocation.

1890 Sitting Bull is killed at Standing Rock reservation by American Indian police hired by the United States.

1890 Sioux chief Big Foot and many of his tribe are killed in the Massacre of Wounded Knee. This ends the Sioux's struggle for their homelands.

Buffalo coin

1924 United States citizenship granted to American Indians and marked by a coin bearing a buffalo.

Ghost dance shirt

1870

1924

Nomadic Life

MANY TRIBES, such as the Cheyenne and Arapaho of the Great Plains, were nomadic. Their life was regulated by the bison who supplied them with their food, clothing and shelter. There were also semi-nomadic tribes such as the Pawnee, who spent part of their time in permanent lodges but sometimes wandered onto the Plains to hunt bison. Others, like the Inuit in the Arctic and the Pima of the Southwest, lived in villages but moved with the changing seasons. American Indians believed that the land was a source of life, filled with spirits. They lived in harmony with nature, adapting themselves to their surroundings. In contrast, the white settlers believed that they owned the land, and built permanent towns that changed the landscape.

FOLLOWING THE HERD
A hunter on horseback catches up with two bison. Before the 1700s, there were massive herds of bison. The Great Plains were virtually treeless, with vast areas of grass to feed the large animals. The Plains covered an area of about 750 mi. by 1,250 mi. and hunters often had to travel for days to glimpse a herd.

FREE LIVING ON THE PLAINS
Groups of women and children moving home across the Great Plains were a common sight. The men would often travel behind the convoy to guard the families from surprise attacks. A travois (carrying frame) was one of the most effective ways of carrying tepees and clothes. It was simply two long poles tied together. Bundles of possessions were strapped in the center, and sometimes children sat on it.

MAKE A TEPEE
You will need: an old double sheet (or fabric measuring approx 8 x 3 ft), scissors, pencil, ruler/tape measure, large and small paintbrushes, yellow, blue and red acrylic paints, water bowl, 12 bamboo sticks 10 ft long, rope or string, three small sticks, large stones (optional).

1 Lay the sheet flat. In the center of one longer edge, cut a semicircle 18 in. across and 8 in. deep. Cut the fabric into a semicircle 5 ft deep all around.

2 Measure, then make, three evenly spaced small holes on each of the straight edges. Start 2½ in. in from the center and 1 in. in from the flat edge.

3 Using a pencil and ruler, draw a geometrical pattern of triangles, lines and circles. Make it bold and simple. Paint it, then let dry.

CAMPING ON THE SHORES OF LAKE HURON

A group of Ojibwas go about their everyday business in a camp by Lake Huron. A woman is pounding corn in preparation for making corn mush. The men are resting by their birchbark canoes after a fishing trip. Their simple home is a conical form of the birchbark wigwam. Families would always try to pitch their homes near water.

WHALE KNIFE

This knife has a bone spear tip and shell blades. It was used by the Makah and Nootka whale hunters of the Northwest Coast who used it to cut blubber off whales.

TREASURED MEMORIES

An Arctic Inuit carved pictures on a walrus's tusk to record a great day of hunting caribou. Color was added by rubbing a mixture of charcoal and grease into the etched lines.

MOVING ON

This family of Blackfoot Indians are migrating to Canada. They have few possessions. The homes of the nomadic tribes were easy to construct and easy to pack when it was time to move on.

Your tepee is a simplified version of the Plains tepees. These were large, heavy constructions made of buffalo skin. They had a built-in smoke flap and a cut-out hole for the door.

4 Take three of the bamboo sticks and join them together at the top. Arrange them on the ground to form a tripod. Tie them securely.

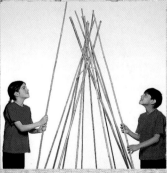

5 One by one, lean the rest of the bamboo sticks against and around the tripod. Remember to leave a gap which will be your tepee entrance.

6 Now take the painted sheet (your tepee cover) and wrap it around the frame. Overlap the two sides at the top of the frame so that the holes join up.

7 Insert a small stick through the two top holes to join them. Do this for each of the other holes. Place stones around the bottom to secure your tepee.

Travel and Transport

NORTH AMERICAN INDIANS were often on the move, although walking was at first their only form of land transport. Hunting and trade were the main reasons for traveling. Young infants were carried in cradleboards, while Inuit babies were put into the hoods of their mothers' parkas. Travois were popular among those living on the Plains. These were frames dragged by dogs and later, horses. One strong dog could pull a load of 50 pounds. In the late 1600s, the Spanish introduced horses, which the Crees called big dogs. This transformed Plains life, as tribes could travel greater distances to fresh hunting grounds.

WATER WAYS
A Kutenai Indian uses his birchbark canoe to paddle out to a clump of rushes. Much of North America is covered with rivers, streams and lakes, and tribesmen were skilled boatbuilders. There were kayaks (Arctic), bark canoes (Woodlands) and large cedar canoes (Northwest Coast).

ANCIENT TRACKS
Traveling over land was traditionally by foot. American Indians made carrying pouches from animal skins, which were tied to their backs by leather strips. For thousands of years, ancient trade routes connected villages that were hundreds of miles apart. Paths and trails were mainly formed by animals, either migrating or looking for food and water. Hunters found and used these trails, which were often no bigger than the width of one person.

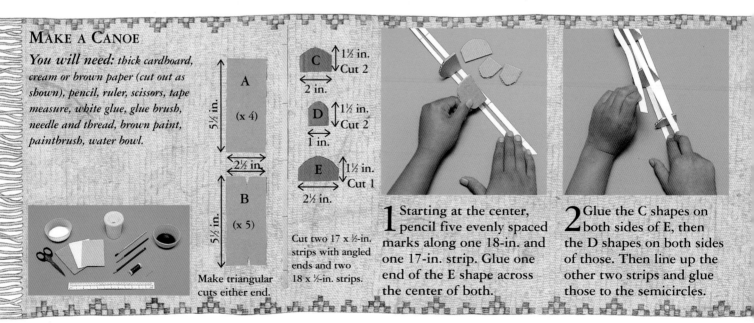

MAKE A CANOE
You will need: thick cardboard, cream or brown paper (cut out as shown), pencil, ruler, scissors, tape measure, white glue, glue brush, needle and thread, brown paint, paintbrush, water bowl.

A (x 4) — 5½ in. — 2½ in.

B (x 5) — 5½ in.

Make triangular cuts either end.

C — 1½ in. — Cut 2 — 2 in.

D — 1½ in. — Cut 2 — 1 in.

E — 1½ in. — Cut 1 — 2½ in.

Cut two 17 x ½-in. strips with angled ends and two 18 x ½-in. strips.

1 Starting at the center, pencil five evenly spaced marks along one 18-in. and one 17-in. strip. Glue one end of the E shape across the center of both.

2 Glue the C shapes on both sides of E, then the D shapes on both sides of those. Then line up the other two strips and glue those to the semicircles.

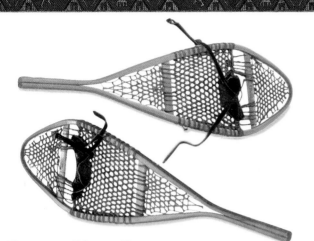

KEEPING YOUR BALANCE
In the north, walking on snow was aided by snowshoes, so that even in deep snow a hunter could pursue his prey. Inuit, in the Subarctic and Arctic, used test sticks, similar to ski poles, to test the strength of ice.

TRAVOIS TRAVEL
Chief Eagle Calf is getting ready for a trip. The long poles of the travois are made into a V–shape and attached to the horse's saddle with leather thongs. The open ends drag on the ground. A carrying platform made of animal skin is stretched across the middle and lashed to the frame. This could be piled with goods or children. It took two horses to carry the poles and covers of a single tepee.

SLEDDING
Sleds were essential in ice and snow. Runners were made of wood or whalebone with antlers for crosspieces. Strips of rawhide helped to cushion the rider and make the ride less bumpy. Sleds were pulled by husky dogs either singly or in teams of up to eight.

COLD HOMECOMING
In the snowy Arctic, Inuit used dogs to pull sleds. Dogs were no use over ice floes, so the Inuit pulled his own sled.

Birchbark canoes were made by the Chipewyan tribe in the Subarctic. They were used for crossing lakes and streams, but also for fishing, farming and gathering rushes and wild rice.

3 Glue the two 18-in. strips together, then the two 17-in. strips, at both ends. Glue shapes B to the frame, making sure the triangular cuts fit over C, D and E.

4 Neaten the ends by gluing the excess paper around the frame. Place the A shapes over the gaps, then glue to the top of the frame.

5 Continue sticking on the rectangles of paper, until all of the boat is covered. Now, carefully fold over and glue the tops of the paper all around.

6 Thread the needle. Using an overlapping stitch, sew all around the top edge of the boat to secure the flaps. Now you can paint your boat.

Tribal Society

A SINGLE TRIBE COULD BE AS SMALL as ten families or stretch to thousands. Neighboring tribes would come together in times of war, for ceremonies and for trading, or to form powerful confederacies (unions). Some Algonquin people formed the Powhatan Confederacy, named after their leader, and controlled the coastal region of present-day Virginia.

Other northeastern groups formed the League of the Iroquois to prevent conflict between local tribes. In the Southeast, the Creek, Seminole, Cherokee, Choctaw and Chickasaw were known by Europeans as the Five Civilized Tribes because of their system of law courts and land rights developed from European influences.

MAGNIFICENTLY COSTUMED
American Horse of the Oglala Sioux wears a double-trail war headdress. His painted shirt shows he was a member of the Ogle Tanka'un, or Shirt Wearers, who were wise and brave.

COMMITTEE MEETING
A Sioux council gathers to hear the head chief speak. Councils were made up of several leaders or chiefs. They elected the head chief, whose authority came from his knowledge of tribal lore and skill as a warrior.

MAKE A HEADDRESS
You will need: ruler, 3 ft x ½-in. red ribbon, red upholstery tape (30 x 2½ in.), masking tape, needle, cotton string, scissors, white paper, black paint, paintbrushes, water bowl, 3mm diameter balsa dowel, white glue, 6 feathers (optional), white, red, yellow, light and dark blue felt, beads (optional), red paper, 8 x ½-in. lengths of colored ribbon.

1 Lay the 3-ft length of red ribbon along the middle of the upholstery tape. Leave 5-in. lengths at each end. Tape it in place while you sew it on.

2 Next, make the feathers. Cut 26 feathers from the white paper. They need to be 7 in. long and 1½ in. at their widest point. Paint the tips black.

3 When the black paint is dry, use the scissors to make tiny cuts around the edges of the paper feathers. This will make the paper look more like feathers.

WOMEN IN SOCIETY

The Iroquois women attended council meetings, but in most tribes women did not join councils or become warriors. Women held a respected place in society. In many tribes, such as the Algonquian, people traced their descent through their mother. When a man married, he left his home to live with his wife's family.

DISPLAYS OF WEALTH

Potlatch ceremonies could last for several days. The gathering was a lavish feast celebrated by tribes on the Northwest Coast. Gifts would be exchanged and the status of a tribe judged by their value.

IN COMMAND

This chief comes from the Kainah group of Blackfoot Indians. The Kainah were also known by Europeans as the Blood Indians because of the red face paint they wore. The Blackfoot headdress had feathers that stood upright as opposed to the Sioux headdress, which sloped backward sometimes, with trailing eagle feathers.

FEATHER PIPE OF PEACE

North American Indians had a long tradition of smoking pipes. Plants were often smoked for religious and ritual reasons. Early peace talks involved passing around a pipe for all to smoke to show they had good intentions of keeping agreements.

4 Cut the balsa dowel into 26 lengths of 5½ in. long. Carefully glue a stick to the center of the back of each feather, starting just below the black tips.

5 If you are also using real bird feathers, tie them with cotton to the bottom of six of the paper feathers. These will be at the front of the headdress.

6 Glue and tape the feathers to the front of the red band, overlapping the feathers slightly. Position them so that the six real feathers are in the center.

7 Cut ½ x 2½-in. lengths of white felt. Glue them over each of the sticks.

Instructions for the headdress continue on the next page...

Dress and Identity

ONE OF THE MOST POPULAR images of a North American Indian is that of a warrior dressed in fringed buckskin with a war headdress and decorated with body paint and beads. That was just one style of dress mainly used by the Plains Indians. Each nation, or tribe, had its own identity and distinctive clothing. Hunters dressed in animal skins and furs.

In areas where agriculture dominated, cloth was woven from wild plant fiber or cultivated cotton. Tribes, such as the Navajo, began to use wool when the Spanish introduced sheep in the 1600s. Climate also dictated what was worn. In the cold north, the Inuit wore mittens, boots and hooded coats called parkas. These were made of seal or caribou skins with the fur worn on the inside. Many east coast and Woodlands men wore just loin cloths or leggings, while women wore fringed skirts.

HOPI GIRL
The squash-blossom hairstyle of this Hopi girl tells us that she is single. It was a symbol of maturity and readiness for marriage. Married women wore their hair loose or in braids. Hopi men wove cotton for blankets and clothes. The women would dye them.

NATURAL COLORS
North American Indians made natural dyes and stains from the plants around them. Vivid reds, yellows, blues and greens could be produced by squeezing and grinding berries and nuts. Leaves and bark were also used.

blackberries

walnuts

raspberries

8 Cut out ½ x ⅓-in. pieces of red felt. Cut 3 for 10 of the feathers (5 each end) and 2 for the rest. Glue to the white felt to make stripes.

9 Cut out a 16 x 1½-in. yellow felt band. Decorate it by gluing on triangles of light and dark blue felt, and small squares of red felt.

10 You can also decorate it with beads. Carefully glue these onto the centerpiece, in the middle of the felt squares and triangles.

11 Very carefully glue the centerpiece to the red band, using a ruler to help you place it in the middle. Some feathers will show on either side.

TRADITIONAL CRAFTS
This woman wears a modern version of a cape. Woodlands and Plains people particularly liked the red and blue cloth brought by European traders.

BEADED VEST
To decorate this man's vest the Sioux would have traded goods for glass beads brought to North America from Italy. Beads were traded by weight or by length, in strings. Before beads, the Sioux used porcupine quills to decorate their ceremonial dress.

WORN WITH PRIDE
Scalplocks of human hair hang down the front of this hide shirt. These show that the Plains warrior who owned it had surpassed himself in battle. He would wear it with pride on ceremonial occasions. The shirt has been made from two deerskins stitched together.

Plains warriors had to earn the right to wear a headdress like this. Such a long and elaborate war headdress would not usually be worn into battle, but kept for ceremonial occasions.

VERSATILE HAT
This early, woven spruce-root hat was worn by the Nootka on the Northwest Coast. It could also be used for carrying, storage or even as a fish trap. To make it, bundles of fiber were woven together, then coiled into a spiral shape.

12 Draw a circle 1 in. in diameter on the red paper. Then draw a 6-in. tail starting at the circle. It should measure ½ in. across and taper to a point.

13 Draw eight of these and cut them out. Glue them to the ends of the feathers on the middle of the band so that the points stick into the air.

14 Cut out two circles of yellow felt, 2 in. in diameter, and decorate with red and white felt shapes. Glue the colored ribbons to the back of the circles.

15 Finally, glue or stitch the felt circles on to the headdress on top of the decorative band. The ribbons should hang down on either side of your ears.

Ornament and Decoration

JEWELRY, BODY PAINT and tattoos were worn by both men and women. Haida women tattooed their faces, bodies and the backs of their hands with family symbols. The people of the Yuma wore minimal clothing so that they could display their tattoos with pride. Tattoos could be simple or elaborate, such as the designs that decorated Timucua adults. These were colored black, red and blue. A tattoo revealed status or was worn to gain protection from a spirit. A less permanent and painful form of skin decoration was created with face and body paints. Hairstyles also carried meanings. A particular style could indicate that a young man was unmarried, belonged to a military society or was a brave warrior. Woodlands men had a distinctive hairstyle. They braided their hair at the front and decorated it with turkey feathers. Some Plains warriors, such as the Pawnee and Iowa, shaved their heads completely, leaving a long tuft on top.

WAR PAINT
Mato-Tope, the chief of the Mandan people, put on his war paint just to have his picture painted. He was posing for the artist Karl Bodmer in 1834. Body paint was used to indicate a social position, and was usually applied for ceremonies and before going to war.

CHILDREN'S COSTUMES
These children were photographed in 1913. Even without being told the date, their costume gives away the era and the tribe they are from. This style of clothes was worn by the Sioux. The girl's hair is braided with a center part. This was known as the reservation style because it was popular after the tribe had been moved to official camps. Children's dress was usually a smaller version of adults' clothing.

MAKE A NECKLACE
You will need: white paper, ruler, white glue, brush for the glue, paints in blue, turquoise and red, paintbrush, water bowl, scissors, air-drying modeling clay, wooden skewer, string.

1 Roll up strips of thin white paper into ¼-in. tubes. Glue down the outer edge to seal the tube and let dry. Make three of these paper tubes.

2 Paint the rolls of paper. Paint one roll blue, one turquoise and one red, making sure that you cover all the white. Let them dry.

3 When dried, the painted paper tubes will have hardened slightly. Carefully cut the tubes into ½-in. pieces to make little beads.

THE NATURAL LOOK

Body paints were extracted from raw materials. Red came from earth with iron in it, and copper ore was used for green and blue. Charcoal made a good black. Berries were used to stain faces and clothes.

ocher

charcoal

blueberries

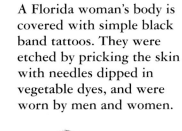

MEDICINE MAN

This medicine man from New Mexico is wearing a head wrap. His beads, scarf and particularly the blanket wrap were popular among the Diné (Navajos). Other tribes wore head wraps, such as the Osage, who wore an otter-skin turban.

TATTOOED WOMAN

A Florida woman's body is covered with simple black band tattoos. They were etched by pricking the skin with needles dipped in vegetable dyes, and were worn by men and women.

DECORATIVE TEETH

An Inuit has carved ivory ornaments for this necklace. Ivory comes from the tusks (canine teeth) of the walrus or the sperm whale.
Inuits use ivory as well as wood, bone, fur and feathers for jewelry, ceremonial masks and trinkets.

Native craftmakers traditionally made beads like these from bone, stone and shell. Some of their bone beads were 3–4 in. long. It was the European traders who brought glass beads over in the 1500s.

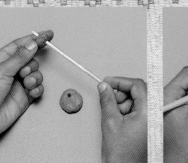

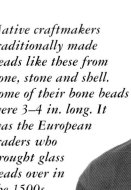

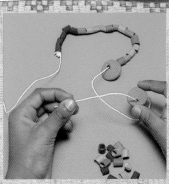

4 Make two larger clay beads by rolling the clay on a flat surface. When you are happy with their shape, pierce the center with the skewer.

5 Let the clay beads dry and harden. When they are ready, paint both of the beads blue (or your preferred color). Once again, let them dry.

6 Thread the beads onto the string. Start with the clay beads, which will hang in the centre. Then, add the blue on either side, then turquoise, then red.

7 Tie a large loop knot at each end of the string when you have finished threading, to stop the beads from falling off. Your necklace is ready to wear.

Native American Homes

During the winter months, the Inuit of the far north built their dome-shaped homes out of blocks of ice or with hard soil, wood and whale bones. Houses had to be adapted to their surroundings. Where wood was plentiful in the east, a variety of homes was built. The wikiup, or wigwam, was dome-shaped and made out of thatch, bark or hide, tightly woven across an arch of bent branches. Basic, rectangular thatched houses were built from a construction of chopped twigs covered with a mixture of clay and straw, or mud. Near the east coast, massive longhouses, up to 150 feet long, with a barrel-shaped roof, were made from local trees. Some tribes lived in different kinds of shelters depending on the season. The Plains Indians mostly lived in tepees (tents made of hide) or sometimes in earth lodges. The most similar to modern buildings were the homes of the Pueblos in the Southwest. These were terraced villages built of bricks made of mud. The Pueblo Indians also built round underground ceremonial chambers with a hidden entrance in the roof.

At Home
A Mandan chief relaxes with his family and dogs inside his lodge. Notice how a hole is cut in the roof to let out smoke from the fire and let fresh air in. Earth lodges were popular with Mandan and Hidatsa people on the Upper Missouri River. The layout followed strict customs. The family would sleep on the south side, guests slept on the north. Stores and weapons were stored at the back. The owner of this home has his horse inside to prevent it from being stolen while the family sleeps.

Homes on the Plains
The hides of around 12 buffaloes were used to cover a family tepee belonging to a Plains Indian. Tepee comes from a Siouan word meaning to dwell. Hides were sewn together and stretched over wooden poles about 25 ft high. When it became too hot inside, the tepee sides were rolled up. In winter, a fire was lit in the center.

Totem Pole
Totem poles were usually found in the far northwest of the United States. They were carved out of wood, often from the mighty thuja (red cedar) trees. Tall totem poles were erected outside the long plank houses of the Haida people. These homes were shared by several families. The poles were carved and painted to keep a record of the family histories of the people inside. They were also sometimes made to honor a great chief.

EARTH LODGES

Mandan Indians perform the Buffalo Dance in front of their lodges. These were built by using logs to create a dome frame, which was then covered over with tightly packed earth.

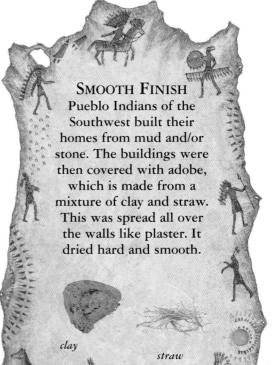

SMOOTH FINISH

Pueblo Indians of the Southwest built their homes from mud and/or stone. The buildings were then covered with adobe, which is made from a mixture of clay and straw. This was spread all over the walls like plaster. It dried hard and smooth.

clay

straw

LAYERS OF BRICK

This ruin was once part of a complex of buildings belonging to Pueblo Indians. Pueblo homes were often many-storied with flat roofs. The floors were reached by ladders. Circular brick chambers were built underground. These were the kivas used for religious and ceremonial rites.

oles in the
oof to let
ut smoke

THE LONGHOUSE

Iroquois people of the Woodlands built long wooden houses. The frame was made of poles hewn from tree trunks with cladding made from sheets of thick bark. Homes were communal. Many families lived in one longhouse, each with their own section built around an open fire.

sleeping platform

higher platform
for storing food

Groups of longhouses were built together, sometimes inside a protective fence.

Family Life

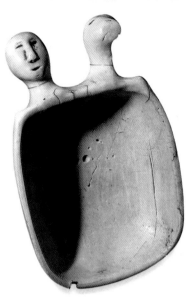

R OLES WITHIN THE FAMILY were well-defined. The men were the hunters, protectors and tribal leaders. Women tended crops, made clothes, cared for the home and the sick, and prepared the food. The children's early days were carefree, but they quickly learned to respect their elders. From an early age, young girls were taught the skills of craftwork and homemaking by their mothers, while the boys learned to use weapons and hunt from the men. Girls as young as 12 years old could be married. Boys had to exchange presents with their future in-laws before the marriage was allowed to take place. At birth most children were named by a grandparent. Later, as adults, they could choose another name of their own.

BONES FOR DINNER
This spoon was carved from animal bone. For the early family there were no metal utensils. Many items were made from bone, tusks, antlers or horns. Bone was also used to make bowls.

A DAY'S HUNTING
Blackfoot girls look on as men leave camp on a hunting trip. They are in search of bison. If the hunt is successful, the women will help skin the animals, then stretch out the hide to dry. Bison skins were used to make tepee covers. Softer buckskin, from deer, was used for clothing.

HOLDING THE BABY
A woman holds her baby strapped to a cradleboard. Domestic scenes were often the focus of American Indian crafts, reflecting the importance of family life.

MAKE A KACHINA DOLL
You will need: cardboard roll, ruler, scissors, compass, pencil, thick cardboard, white glue, brush for glue, masking tape, paints in cream/yellow, green/blue, red and black, paintbrush, water bowl, red paper.

1 Take the cardboard roll and cut a section of about 1½ in. (or a third) off the top. This will form the head piece. The larger end will form the body.

2 Use the compass (or end of the cardboard roll) to draw four circles of ½-in. radius on cardboard. Then draw a smaller circle ¾-in. radius. Cut them all out.

3 Glue the larger circles to either end of both of the cardboard roll tubes. Let dry. Glue the smaller circle of cardboard on top of one end of the longer roll.

ROLE PLAY

Children love to copy their elders, and this little Sioux girl is wearing an adult's large headdress. She is holding a favorite doll to pose for the picture. Playing with dolls taught girls about their future role as a care-giver. Boys were taught to ride, shoot arrows and hunt.

FAMILY GATHERING

A Cree family in Canada enjoys a quiet evening around the fire. American Indian families were usually small, as no more than two or three children survived the harsh life. However, a lodge was often home to an extended family. There could be two or three sisters, their families and grandparents under one roof.

Kachina dolls were made by the Hopi people to represent different spirits. This is the Corn kachina. Some parents gave the dolls to their children to help them learn about tribal customs.

BABY CARRIER

For the first year of its life, a baby would spend its time strapped to a cradleboard, such as this one influenced by the eastern Woodland tribes. It was also used by eastern Sioux, Iowa, Pawnee and Osage parents. A baby could sleep or be carried in safety while laced in its cradle, leaving the mother free to work. The board was strapped to the mother's back.

4 The smaller cardboard circle forms the doll's neck. Glue the small cardboard roll (the head) on top of the larger cardboard roll (the body).

5 Cut two small L-shapes from cardboard to form the arms. Then cut two small ear shapes from the cardboard. Cover these shapes with masking tape.

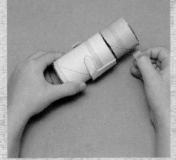

6 Glue the arms to the body and the ears to the sides of the head, so that they stick out at right angles. Paint the doll the colors shown above.

7 While the paint is drying, cut two small feather shapes from red paper. Glue these to the top of the doll's head, so that they stick into the air.

Food and Farming

FROM THE NORTH AMERICAN Indians' earliest days, tribes have hunted, fished and gathered their own food. Archaeologists recently found evidence of a version of popcorn dating back to 4000 B.C. The area and environment tribes lived in determined their lifestyle. Inuit and coastal people fished and hunted. Calusas in Florida farmed the sea, sectioning off areas for shellfish. Tribes on the Northwest Coast took their food from the sea and so had little reason to develop farming, although they did grow tobacco. For many tribes, however, farming was an important way of life, and each developed its own agricultural skills.

The Secotan tribal name means an area that is burnt, referring to their method of setting fire to land to clear it for farming. They and other tribes on the fertile east coast planted thriving vegetable gardens. As well as the staple corn, squash and beans, they grew tomatoes, berries, vanilla beans and asparagus.

FOOD BASKET
The Apaches and other people in the Southwest are renowned for making beautiful baskets. They waterproofed them with melted pinon (pine tree) gum. Versatile basket bowls were used for storing corn and carrying or serving food.

COOKING OUTSIDE
This beehive-shaped structure is a traditional outdoor oven. It was used by the Pueblo and other people of the Southwest. A fire was lit inside the dome, which heated stones placed all around the fire. The oven was used to bake corn bread or roast vegetables and meat.

MAKE CORN CAKES
You will need: *7 oz corn tortilla flour or all-purpose flour, scale, sieve (optional), mixing bowl, cold water, pitcher, metal spoon, wooden or cutting board, rolling pin, frying pan, a little oil for cooking, honey.*

1 Measure out 7 oz of flour on the scale. Carefully pour (or sieve) the flour into the mixing bowl. Fill the pitcher with fresh, cold water.

2 Slowly add the water to the flour in the bowl. Add a little at a time, stirring constantly as you pour, until the mixture forms a stiff dough.

3 Using your hands, gently knead (press) the mixture. Keep kneading until the dough is not too sticky. You may need to add a little more flour.

BAGGING WILD RICE

Two rice gatherers are sorting their harvest of rice just as their ancestors would have done. Vast areas of wild rice grew on the shores of lakes and rivers of the eastern Woodlands. Men and women would gather the stalks, bend them over the edge of a boat and strike them with a blunt tool. The grains of rice would fall into the boat. They were then gathered in bags to dry in the sun.

THREE SISTERS

Corn was part of the diet of most tribes. It was grown as early as A.D. 200. The two other important crops were squash and beans. These three crops were known by the Iroquois as the Three Sisters.

squash *corn*

beans

PREPARING A MEAL

These Secotan people are sorting beans for a meal. American Indians grew about 60 different types of beans. Most tribes would prepare food to share.

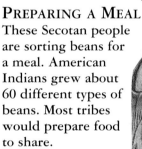

FISH SUPPER

It was a good day's fishing for this Inuit. The fish will be hung up to be smoked and preserved. Inuit caught fish from kayaks or trapped fish in shallow water. In winter they fished through holes in the ice.

Tortillas were often eaten with beans and savory food. They also taste delicious with honey. Try them!

4 Sprinkle flour on the board. Take the dough from the bowl and knead it on the floured board for about 10 minutes. Let it stand for 30 minutes.

5 Pull off a small lump of dough. Roll it between your hands to form a flat round ball. Repeat this process until you have used all the dough.

6 Keep patting the dough balls until they form flat round shapes. Finish by using the rolling pin to roll them into flat, thin cakes, also known as tortillas.

7 Ask an adult to come and cook them with you. Heat a heavy frying pan or griddle. Gently cook the tortillas until they are lightly browned on both sides.

Hunting

THE EXCITING BUT DANGEROUS TASK of chasing the herds began only after a buffalo dance had been performed. The first signs of the bison (the real name for American buffalo) were often tracks left in the earth. Hunters followed these until the herd was spotted in the distance. Early hunters stalked the animals on foot, which was very dangerous. They made an avenue out of rocks and bushes down which the bison were driven. This lead to a jump where the animals were stampeded to the edge of a steep cliff to fall to their death. When the horse came, it made hunting easier, though not always safer. A hunter had to ride in close to the herd, pick out a bison and drive it away. Bison was not the only animal hunted. The rivers to the east were once rich in beaver, much favored by fur traders, and tribes in California would hunt deer in the hills.

BUFFALO GRAVEYARD
The skulls were all that was left of the bison after a hunt. Meat was used for food, fat for glue and soup, and the hide became tepees and moccasins. Bladder and bones were made into cooking utensils, and the hair was used as stuffing.

HUNTING BEAR
This painting by George Catlin shows grizzly bears being speared by Plains warriors. Bears were sacred animals to many tribes, however, and believed to be guardian spirits. A warrior might paint symbols of the bear on his shield or red claw marks on his face for protection.

MAKE A SKIN ROBE

You will need: *an old single sheet (or large piece of thin cotton fabric), scissors, tape measure or ruler, pencil, large needle, brown thread, felt in red, yellow, dark blue and light blue, white glue, glue brush, black embroidery floss (or string), red cotton thread (or other color).*

1 Take the sheet and cut out a rectangle 5 x 2 ft. Then cut out two 16 x 14-in. rectangles for the arms. Fold the main (body) piece in half.

2 At the center of the fold, draw a neckline 9 in. across and 3 in. deep. Cut it out. Roll fabric over at shoulders and stitch down with an overlapping stitch.

3 Open the body fabric out flat and line up the arm pieces, with the center on the stitched ridge. Stitch the top edge of the arm pieces onto the body.

FOOLING THE BUFFALO

Hunters have disguised themselves as wolves to sneak up close to the bison. The skin masked the hunter's own body smell, and they often tried to imitate a wolf's movements. It was essential to keep downwind because of the bison's keen sense of smell. However, the bison had very poor eyesight.

BUFFALO RUN

Hunters on horses rush at a bison trying to force it toward archers lying in wait. On a hunt, the first goal was to get all the animals to run in a circle. Then the hunters would surround them killing individual animals until they had all the meat needed. If the bison stampeded, the chase continued.

The North American Indians would have made their robes from buckskin. When the Europeans first spotted the natives wearing it, they could not figure out what the pale, soft material was made from.

BUTCHERS AT WORK

A hunt is over, and the tribe moves in to skin and butcher the kill. Often it was the women and elder children who handled the harvesting. The skin would carefully be taken off in one piece and used to make clothing. Meat would be prepared for a feast.

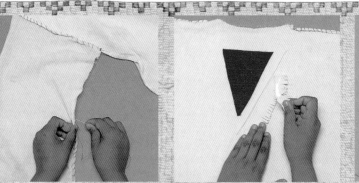

4 Fold the fabric in half again to see the shirt's shape. Now stitch the undersides of the sleeves. The sides of the shirt were usually not sewn together.

5 Your shirt is ready to decorate. Cut out strips and triangles of felt and glue them to the shirt. Make fringes by cutting into one side of a felt strip.

6 Make fake hair pieces by cutting 3-in. lengths of black thread and tying them together in bunches. Wind red thread tightly around the top, as here.

7 Glue or sew the fake hair (or scalplocks) on to your shirt. You can follow the pattern we used as shown in the picture (top), or create your own.

The Mighty Bison

FOR GENERATIONS, THE NATIVE bison (or buffalo) provided the Plains Indians with most of life's essentials, such as their food and housing materials. Although they hunted all year round, summer and autumn were the main buffalo seasons. During the summer months, large herds of thousands of animals came to the grass ranges to fatten up for winter. The arrival of the bison was marked by festive ceremonies before hunting began. The night after a successful hunt, a large feast was held with singing and dancing. A great deal of bison meat was eaten at the feast, but some had to be preserved for harder times. For this the meat was cut into narrow strips and hung over wooden racks to dry in the sun or over a fire. This is called jerky. Tougher meat was ground and mixed with bison fat and berries, a delicacy known as pemmican.

BUFFALO DANCE
Mandan men are getting themselves in the right mood for a hunt. Buffalo dances were held to bring the hunters good luck. Legend has it that the bison taught men their dance and chant. The Plains Indians believed in many spirits. They felt that if they prayed and chanted, the spirits would help them. The bull (male) head and hide robes were sacred objects worn by the shamans (medicine men) and those offering up prayers for the hunt.

OFFERING A PRAYER
A lone American Indian stands on top of the hill. He is using the sacred skull of a buffalo to call upon the great spirit of Wakan Tanka to bring buffalo herds to the Great Plains. The Sioux believed their world was full of spirits that controlled the earth, the sun, the sky, the wind—in fact, everything. Wakan Tanka controlled all of the spirits.

HUNTER VERSUS THE BISON
A large bull (male) turns on his attacker. An average male weighed more than a ton and stood more than 5 ft high at the shoulder. The lone rider is armed with a spear and guides his horse with knee pressure alone. A hunt was a chance for a warrior to prove himself. If he killed a bison, a hunter had the honor of eating the heart. The American Indians believed that this transferred the bison's spiritual power to the hunter.

STRETCHING THE HIDE
An Oklahoma man is stretching and tanning the hide in a traditional way. North American Indians stretched buffalo skin over a wooden frame or staked it out on the ground. First, the fat, flesh and fur had to be scraped off, then the skin was washed with a mixture of grease and water. Sometimes urine was used. Rawhide, the uncured animal skin with its fur scraped off, was used to make drums, shields and robes.

A HUNT GOES ON
The excitement of bison hunting is captured in this Blackfoot painting on a tepee lining. Pictures were used to record significant events in tribal life. They were painted on tepees or shields. The images described war exploits, good hunting trips or the family history. The bison here were probably eaten by the tribe.

WILD AND FREE
In 1800, there were an estimated 60 million bison roaming the Plains. These numbers fell dramatically as European settlers moved further west. Around four million bison were slaughtered in just four years. They were hunted almost to extinction. In 1872, Yellowstone National Park was the first conservation area set up to protect them.

HUNTING AS SPORT
Passengers on the Kansas Pacific Railroad shoot buffalo for sport. When railways were built in 1860, white settlers moved west of the Mississippi River and onto the Plains. They did not understand the American Indians' way of life and killed many animals, including bison. Later, the United States government encouraged white hunters to shoot herds. They thought that if the bison were destroyed, tribes would lose their livelihood and give up their land.

Language and Communication

DIFFERENT TRIBES USUALLY SPOKE widely differing languages. It is estimated that at one time more than 500 languages in 2,200 different dialects were spoken. There were a few who shared similar tongues. The seven Sioux sub-tribes spoke a Siouan language, while the Plains Crees, Ojibwas, Blackfoot and Arapaho spoke Algonquian languages. These tribes were, however, spread over a wide area, which made inter-tribal communication very difficult. The North American Indians also developed a sign language using hand gestures for inter-tribal communication. Before the Europeans arrived, there was no written alphabet. Instead, they used pictographs, which are drawings representing humans, animals or objects. An alphabet was created by Sequoya of the Cherokees in 1821 and, once accepted by the elders, it was passed on to the people. In 1828, the Cherokee Phoenix newspaper was published in Cherokee and English.

REVEALING DREAMS
These glyphs have been painted by the Chippewa people of the Woodlands. Each picture is symbolic, based on mythical figures rather than signifying real events. They were either spirits worshipped by the tribe or images the artist saw in a dream.

PAINTING ON SKIN
An elderly tribal member is painting on a buffalo skin. The dried skin was pegged out on the ground and stretched taut. The tools were sticks dipped in paints or dyes made from plants and earth. Black, yellows and reds were the most common. European traders later introduced oils, poster paints and watercolors. Hide was not the only place pictures and glyphs were painted. Records were stored on bark, bone, totem poles, and later, cloth, while Inuit carved pictographs on tusks.

MAKE A WINTER COUNT
You will need: muslin, piece of cardboard or a board, masking tape, ruler, pencil, scissors, white glue, brush for glue, sheet of 8½ x 11-in. white paper, tracing paper, thin card stock (preferably cream or white), very fine paintbrush or an ink pen, black ink or paint.

1 Stretch the muslin over a board or piece of cardboard. Tape it down. Draw a 12 x 8-in. rectangle on the muslin. Untape it and cut out the rectangle.

2 Use a brush to paint the cut edges of the muslin with white glue so that they will not fray while you work (and keep them neat afterward).

3 Draw a wide spiral in the middle of the sheet of white paper. Mark 11 points around the line of the spiral. Space the points out evenly.

KEEPING A DIARY

A Plains Indian has recorded a raid by his tribe on another camp. Pictures such as these told the history of a tribe. Some acted as a kind of visual diary and were known as Winter Counts because they were usually made, or added to, in the winter. The family and other tribal members would often gather around telling stories while one wrote them down using picture writing.

SMOKE SIGNAL

Warriors in the Plains region send a smoke signal to the rest of their tribe. A fire of damp leaves or grass would be lit, as it produced heavy smoke. This was allowed to rise in set intervals to convey an agreed message. Sioux warriors sent signals using mirrors to reflect the sun's rays. Woodland tribes developed drum signals and cries.

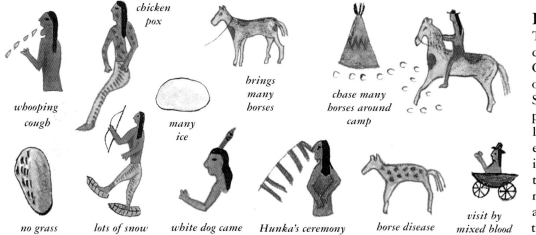

whooping cough   *chicken pox*   *brings many horses*   *chase many horses around camp*

no grass   *many ice*   *lots of snow*   *white dog came*   *Hunka's ceremony*   *horse disease*   *visit by mixed blood*

LIFE ON THE PLAINS

These drawings have been copied from a Sioux Winter Count. Unlike pictographs of the Woodland people, the Sioux Indians painted pictures showing everyday life on the Plains. Such events as bad weather and ill-health greatly affected the tribes. Icy weather meant that plant life and animals were scarce and the tribe might go hungry.

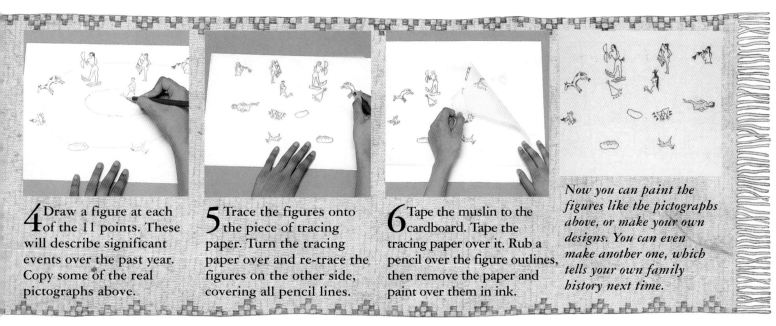

4 Draw a figure at each of the 11 points. These will describe significant events over the past year. Copy some of the real pictographs above.

5 Trace the figures onto the piece of tracing paper. Turn the tracing paper over and re-trace the figures on the other side, covering all pencil lines.

6 Tape the muslin to the cardboard. Tape the tracing paper over it. Rub a pencil over the figure outlines, then remove the paper and paint over them in ink.

Now you can paint the figures like the pictographs above, or make your own designs. You can even make another one, which tells your own family history next time.

Storytelling

NORTH AMERICAN INDIANS LOVED storytelling. Many stories taught the children to respect nature and animals or described social behavior. Stories were also a way of passing on tribal customs, rituals and religious beliefs. Some tribes considered it unlucky to tell tales of mythological events during the summer months. They looked forward to the long winter nights when they would gather in their tepees or lodges and huddle around the fire. Then, they listened to the storyteller, who was often one of the elders. A story might recall past hunts and battles, or it could be a work of complete fiction, although the listener could never be sure, as the tales were always embellished. This was especially true if the storyteller was from the Yuma. The Great Dreams of the Yuma were fantastic tales usually performed as plays and often based on tribal rituals and folklore.

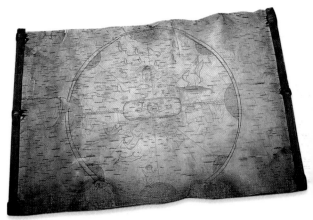

SCROLL OF A SHAMAN
This is a fine example of a birchbark scroll. It is a Midewiwin (Grand Medicine Society) record of the Ojibwa. Most ceremonies were so long and complicated that a chart had to be made to remember all the songs and prayers in the right order. A document such as this was used to record the history and initiation rites of a tribe. Without it, knowledge of them might be lost forever.

STORY BEHIND THE PICTURES
A proud Mandan chief and his wife pose for a picture to be painted. It is not just the chief's headdress that reveals great prowess in battle. The painted skin displayed by the woman tells stories of the tribe's history. The war scenes show that the tribe has been involved in many victorious battles in the past. This group picture was painted between 1833 and 1835 by George Catlin. He was an artist whose paintings of North American Indians are themselves a form of storytelling. They are an important source of information about tribal lives, customs and dress, particularly as the American Indians at that time did not write any books about themselves.

COLORED SAND

Although many tribes made sandpaintings *(shown above),* it was the Navajo who developed the art. The painter trickled powders of yellow, white and red ocher and sandstone into patterns on the sand. Each picture described humans and spirits connected with creation stories and was usually used as part of a healing ceremony.

WRITTEN IN STONE

These children are reading about the history of their ancestors in Colorado Springs. Stone Age North American Indians (the early Pueblo people) carved animals and designs on stone that told a little of their way of life.

HEROIC TALES

The Sioux chief seen at the bottom of this picture must have been exceptionally brave, as his headdress is very long. Painting warrior shields was an ancient art used to pass on tales of battle heroics. This shield may have been painted by one of the warriors involved. Shields were kept in the lodge and brought out when the warrior retold how brave he was. It would be given to his children to keep his memory alive.

THE HISTORIAN

A young boy looks on as his father records tribal stories on dried animal hide. He is already learning the importance of recording the family history. Even in 1903, when this picture was painted, many tribes used picture writing, not the printed word of the white man.

STORY OF LIFE

Totem poles such as this were found mainly on the Northwest Coast. Generally they were carved out of trunks of thuja (red cedar trees) and told tribal or family history. Each face was a mythical creature, an animal protector. Frontal poles stood against Haida homes displaying the crests of the families who lived inside.

Myths and Legends

TRIBAL LIFE WAS FILLED WITH myths and famous tales. Legends of tribal ancestors, gods and spirits were passed down through the generations. Some of the greatest legends were told in song or dance at large gatherings. They were often connected with religious beliefs, and many of the tales were an attempt to explain the origins of the tribes and the universe. The Haida, Snohomish and Quinault (of the Northwest Coast) believed that animals were the original inhabitants of the land. They thought that the coyote (a large wild dog) could take off its fur to reveal a man inside. It was the god Kwatee, who created humans from the coyote. The Iroquois believed in a sky woman and earth goddess named Ataensic. She died giving birth to twins. After her death, one of the twins created the world from her corpse. In Navajo mythology, a sea goddess known as White Shell Woman was in charge of water, and her sister was an earth goddess who made the seasons change each year.

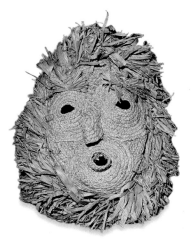

BUSHY HEADS
Members of the Iroquois Husk Face Society wore this type of mask. They were said to have special healing powers and could handle hot ashes and rub them on the heads of patients. The masks were made of braided corn husks and nicknamed bushy heads.

LARGER THAN LIFE
The mighty Thunderbird was a powerful supernatural creature, seen here in a Haida wood carving. A flap of its wings was said to bring thunder, and lightning struck when it blinked. The Algonquins in the east called them Our Grandfathers. They could fight with other beings or grant mighty blessings.

MAKE A SPIRIT MASK
You will need: thick cardboard, scissors, pencil, masking tape, newspaper, all-purpose flour, water, bowl and fork for mixing, fine sandpaper, white and red acrylic paint, paintbrushes, water bowl, awl, elastic, twine, white glue, brush for glue.

1 Cut out an oval piece of cardboard, a little larger than your face. Make four ¾-in. cuts, two toward the top and two at the bottom, as shown above.

2 Overlap the cut bits of card and tape them down. This will create a 3-D shape to fit your face. Ask a friend to help mark holes for eyes and mouth.

3 Cut the eye and mouth holes, then build up the nose, cheeks and mouth. Fold bits of newspaper to make the right shapes and tape them in place.

FISH FACE

An Inuit carved this mask of a fish and its spirit. Inuit and Aleut people wore masks to honor native animals such as the whale, seal, bear and caribou, which were important food sources. The people aimed to please the animal spirits who would ensure good food supplies. Some masks had animal heads with human faces. They were worn for one ceremony, then burned or buried.

SPIRIT MASK

This scary face is an Inuit mask. Creatures in the spirit world were recreated in masks, and so the masks were felt to be alive. Ordinary people wore masks during ceremonies, but shamans wore them more often. A mask carved by a shaman would give him spiritual powers to heal sick people.

SUMMONING SPIRITS

The god of lightning is represented by this kachina doll. Hopi, Zuni and other Pueblo Indians carved many kachina dolls. They were no ordinary dolls—a kachina was a guardian spirit. The Hopi believed the spirits lived in the mountains. They came down on the winter solstice (shortest day of the year) and stayed until the summer solstice (longest day).

LEGEND IN THE MAKING

The pictographs on this Sioux war shield show that the tribe had fought in a huge battle. They are surrounded by the United States Cavalry—the figures around the edges. Many scenes of legendary battles were recorded on shields.

Your mask follows the design of a False Face Mask of the Iroquois. The wearer was a member of a False Face Society and used it during ceremonies to cure the sick.

4 Make a paste of flour and water. Tear bits of newspaper into small strips, dip them into paste and cover the mask with them. Make 2–3 layers.

5 Let the mask dry in a warm place. When dry, smooth it down with sandpaper. Coat in white paint then red, or just several layers of red.

6 When dry, add more detail using white paint. Make a hole on either side using an awl. Tie a piece of elastic to each side to hold the mask on your face.

7 Take the twine and dampen it slightly, then untwist it so you have straw-like strands. Dry them out and glue them to the mask to create hair.

Arts and Crafts

NORTH AMERICAN INDIANS were expert craftsmen and women. Beautiful pots have been found dating back to around 1000 B.C. The people of the Southwest were renowned for their pottery. Black and white Mimbres bowls were known as burial pots because they were broken when their owner died and buried along with the body. Baskets and blankets were the other most important crafts. The ancient Anasazis were known as the basket-making culture because of the

range of baskets they produced. Some were coiled so tightly they could hold water. The Apaches coiled large, flat baskets from willow and plant fibers, and the Paiutes made cone baskets, which were hung on their backs for collecting food. All North American Indians made use of the materials they had on hand such as, wood, bark, shells, porcupine quills, feathers, bones, metals, hide and clay.

BASKET WEAVER
A native Arizona woman is creating a traditional coiled basket. It might be used for holding food or to wear on someone's head. Tlingit and Nootka tribes from the Northwest Coast were among those who wore cone-shaped basket hats.

POTTERY
Zuni people in the Southwest created beautiful pots such as this one. They used baskets as molds for the clay or coiled thin rolls of clay around in a spiral. Afterward, they smoothed out the surface with water. Birds and animals were favorite decorations.

DRILLING WALRUS TUSKS
An Inuit craftsman is working on a piece of ivory. He is using a drill to etch a pattern. The drill bit is kept firmly in place by his chin. This way, his hands are free to move the bow in a sawing action, pushing the drill point into the ivory.

MAKE A TANKARD
You will need: air-drying modeling clay, board, water in bowl, pencil, ruler, cream or white and black poster paints or acrylic paints, fine and ordinary paintbrushes, non-toxic varnish.

1 Roll out a round slab of clay and press it into a flat circle with a diameter of about 4 in. Now, roll out two long sausage shapes of clay.

2 Slightly dampen the edges of the clay circle. Place one end of the clay sausage on the edge of the circle and coil it around. Continue spiralling around.

3 Continue coiling with the other clay sausage. Then, use your dampened fingers to smooth the coils into a good tankard shape and smooth the outside.

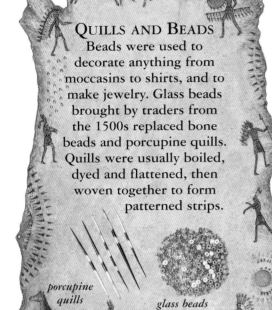

QUILLS AND BEADS

Beads were used to decorate anything from moccasins to shirts, and to make jewelry. Glass beads brought by traders from the 1500s replaced bone beads and porcupine quills. Quills were usually boiled, dyed and flattened, then woven together to form patterned strips.

porcupine quills

glass beads

TALKING BLANKET

It could take half a year for a Tlingit woman to make one of the famous Chilkat blankets. She wove cedar bark fiber and mountain goat wool with her fingers. The Tlingits said that if you knew how to listen, the blankets could talk.

FRUITS OF THE LOOM

Striped blankets were the specialty of Indians in the Southwest. This Hopi woman is using an upright loom made from poles. Pueblo people were the first North American Indians to weave like this.

Each tribe had its own pottery designs and colors. These geometric patterns were common in the Southwest.

4 Roll out another, small sausage shape of clay to make a handle. Dampen the ends and press it onto the clay pot in a handle shape. Let dry out.

5 Using a sharp pencil, mark out the design you want on your tankard. You can follow the traditional Indian pattern or make up your own.

6 Using poster paints or acrylic paints, colour in the pattern on the tankard. Use a fine-tipped brush to create the tiny checked patterns and thin lines.

7 When the paint is dry, coat your tankard in one or two layers of non-toxic varnish using an ordinary paintbrush. This will protect it.

Games and Entertainment

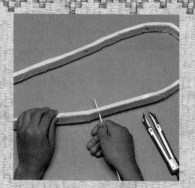

As hard as life was, the North American Indians always found time to relax by playing games and entertaining themselves. There were games of chance and gambling and games of skill. Games of chance included guessing games, dice-throwing, and hand games where one person had to guess in which hand his opponent was hiding marked bones or wooden pieces. Archery, spear throwing and juggling were favorite games to improve hunting skills, and there was a variety of stick and ball games, such as lacrosse. Children also loved to swim and take part in races. In the north, the girls and boys raced on toboggans. Active pastimes like these helped to develop skills a North American Indian needed to survive, such as strength, agility, bravery and stamina. Ritual foot races were also of ceremonial importance. Running could supposedly help the crops grow, bring rain and give renewed strength to the sun.

TEAM GAMES

The Ball Game of the Creek, Seminole, Cherokee and Choctaw people was similar to lacrosse. They used two sticks, while in lacrosse, one is used. Cherokees called it *little brother of war*, and to the Choctaw it was *stickball*.

SNOW FUN

These Inuit children are enjoying a toboggan ride in the snow. They are wrapped up in animal skins. Iroquois adults played Snow Snake to see how far a lance could be slid on ice.

MAKE A LACROSSE STICK

You will need: thick cardboard, ruler or tape measure, pencil, scissors, masking tape, compass, wooden skewer or sharp object to make holes, bamboo stick (to reach to your waist from ground level), white glue, glue brush, string, brown paint, paintbrush, water bowl, light ball.

1 Measure, then cut a strip of cardboard 48 x 1 in. Fold it gently at the center to make a curve (Or cut two 24 x 1 in. pieces and tape them together).

2 Cover the cardboard completely with masking tape. Start from the edges and work around, keeping the bent shape. Cover both sides.

3 Use a compass to mark two points from the center of the bend, 4 in. apart, then two, 4 in. from these and two more 4 in. down. Use a stick to make holes at these points.

GAME OF THE ARROW

Plains tribes enjoy target practice. A stationary target was made of wood, grass or bark. A more adventurous game for the archer was to throw a bundle into the air and try to shoot an arrow into it before it came down. This was a favorite with the Mandan, who tried to shoot several arrows into the air at the same time from one bow.

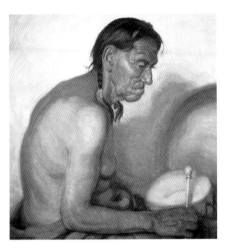

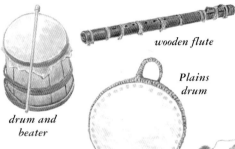

wooden flute

Plains drum

drum and beater

rattle

The aim of the game of lacrosse is to get the leather ball between two posts to score a goal. It is a bit like hockey, but instead of the ball being hit, it is scooped up in the net of the curved stick or racquet.

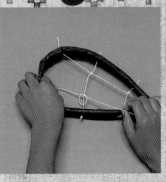

KEEPING THE BEAT

Songs and dance were essential during ceremonies. They inspired visions among listeners, who often chanted to the rhythmic beat.

MUSIC TIME

Instruments were made from everyday materials. Drums were the most important. There were various types of flat or deep drums, mostly made from rawhide (untreated buffalo skin) stretched over a base of carved wood. Reed flutes were sometimes played by Sioux men when they were courting their future wives.

4 Glue the ends of the cardboard strip to the top of the bamboo stick, leaving a loop (as shown above). Tie string around the outside to keep it in place.

5 Pinch the cardboard together at the end of the stick, just under the loop. Tie it tightly with string and trim the ends. Paint the stick brown.

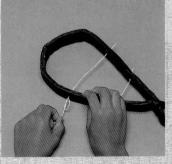

6 When the paint is dry, thread two pieces of string horizontally between the two sets of holes on the sides of the loop. Knot them on the outside.

7 Now, thread two vertical strings. Start at the holes at the top of the frame and tie the string around both horizontal strings. Tie the ends. Use a light ball.

Contact with Europeans

THE VIKINGS WERE THE first Europeans to discover the existence of North America. It was other explorers arriving around 500 years later, however, who created the most impact. These Europeans claimed the land for their own countries, setting up colonies of settlers. They eventually forced many North American Indians from their homelands, killing thousands in the process. When Christopher Columbus landed in the Bahamas in 1492, he set about claiming the land for Spain. Fellow Spaniard Ponce de León landed in Florida in 1512, while Hernando Cortés had conquered the Aztecs in Central America by 1521. Tales of mountains of gold in the Southwest brought a Spanish expedition headed by Vasquez de Coronado. He encountered Apache, Hopi, Pawnee and Wichita Indians. He never did find gold. Sadly, the European explorers and colonists never regarded the American Indians as equals. They tried to force tribes to change their lifestyles, beliefs and even to adapt their traditional crafts to suit European buyers.

EARLY VISITORS
Erik the Red, the Viking king, sailed to Greenland around 982 A.D. He was probably in search of new trading partners. His son Leif later sailed to Newfoundland and established a settlement at a place now called L'Anse aux Meadows. A trade in furs and ivory was set up with northern Europe.

SETTING SAIL
Columbus and his crew prepare to set sail from Spain in 1492 in search of a trade route to India. He never reached Asia but landed on San Salvador in the Bahamas. The Arawaks there thought that Columbus and his men came from the sky and greeted them with praise. Columbus set about claiming the islands for the Spanish Empire, making many of the natives slaves.

A DISTANT LAND

This map from around 1550 shows a crude European impression of North America. Henry II of France ordered Descallier, a royal cartographer (map maker), to make a map of what Central and North America looked like. The French were eager to gain land there for themselves. Jacques Cartier, a French navigator, spent eight years exploring the St. Lawrence River area. He made contact with Huron communities. He wrote and told the king that he hoped the natives would be "easy to tame."

MAN WITH A MISSION

A Plains Indian views a missionary with suspicion. Eastern tribes were the first to meet French missionaries whom they called Black Robes. In California, many were forced to live and work in Spanish mission villages.

SAY A LITTLE PRAYER

Young girls dressed in European clothes have been separated from their families and tribal customs. Europeans could not understand the North American Indians' society and religious beliefs. They wanted to convert them to Christianity, by force if necessary. In many areas, children were taken away from their people and sent to white boarding schools, given European names and taught European religion, language and history.

European Settlers

FROM 1500, NORTH AMERICA was visited by the English, French and Spanish in increasing numbers, each establishing colonies to expand their empires. It was mostly the British and the French who stayed. At first their settlements were on the east coast and in eastern Canada, but gradually they explored further inland, meeting with more and more tribes. Europeans brought diseases previously unknown to the American Indians. The smallpox epidemic of 1837 almost wiped out the Mandan tribe. Fewer than 200 people survived, from a tribe that had once numbered over 2,500. The colonists continued to push out the North American Indians. In the 1760s to 1780s, colonists fought for independence from their empires. In 1783 the United States was officially recognized as being independent from Britain. The United States government wanted to move eastern tribes west of the Mississippi River. They bought the Louisiana Territory in 1803 for 15 million dollars from France. This doubled the size of the United States and marked the end of French rule. It didn't stop there— they continued to push their frontiers west.

LEADING THE WAY

Sacawagea, a Shoshoni girl, guides United States captains Meriwether Lewis and William Clark from Mississippi to the Pacific coast, in 1804. It took them almost one year. President Thomas Jefferson asked them to map out the land from the Mississippi River to the Rockies. This helped to pave the way for settlers to move to the far west.

ROLLING ACROSS THE PLAINS

From around 1850, wagon trains were signs that times were changing for the Plains tribes. Although settlers had been living in North America for around 300 years, they had mostly remained on the east coast. The United States government encouraged white families to move inland.

SOD HOUSE

This is a fine example of a sod house, a house literally made from sod, or turf, cut out of the ground. Settlers had to build homes from whatever material was on hand. Life was hard for the children; they had to do chores, such as feeding chickens. If they were lucky, they went to school.

NEW TOWN

Plains Indians watch a train steaming into a new town. Land was sacred to the tribes who called it their Earth Mother. The settlers thought that the tribes wasted their land and wanted to build towns and railways on it. At first, the federal government took land for settlers. Later, they bought millions of acres of tribal land in various treaties (agreements), using force if the American Indians did not agree.

PANNING FOR GOLD

A man is sifting through sand in search of gold. When gold was discovered in late 1848 in California, it started the Gold Rush. Thousands of immigrants came to the west coast from all over the world. The sheer numbers forced the tribes off their land.

TRAIN ATTACK

Plains warriors attack a train crossing their hunting grounds. The Plains tribes had always been fiercely defensive of their territory. Now they turned on the new invaders. More and more settlers were encouraged to move onto the Plains. In the 1860s, railways were constructed across tribes' lands. These were built over sacred sites and destroyed buffalo hunting grounds which were essential to the tribes' livelihood. Attacks on settlers, trains and white trading posts became more frequent.

Horse Culture

THERE WERE HORSES ROAMING wild in America during prehistoric times, but they had died out by the Ice Age. The Spanish reintroduced the horse to North America in the early 1500s when they brought the animals over on ships. As the Spanish moved north of Mexico further inland, more tribes came to contact with the horse. It was forbidden by Spanish officials to trade in horses, but gradually tribes obtained them one way or another. To go on a horse-stealing raid was counted as a great honor. The arrival of the horse on the Plains had a dramatic effect on tribal life. It meant that they could expand their hunting area, and made hunting bison much easier. It also meant that greater loads could be carried or pulled by horses, including much larger tepees. By 1700, the Crows traded horses with the Colombian Plateau tribes of the Nez Perce, Cayuse and Palouse. The Cayuse became renowned for breeding a strong type of horse, which bears their name. The Palouse were also very good at breeding horses and their name was given to the Appaloosa breed favored by the Nez Perce tribe. Tribes treated the animals with respect, and there was often a special bond between a warrior and his horse.

PLAYING THEIR PART
Horses feature prominently among the many pictures painted by Plains Indians on deer and buffalo skins. On this Blackfoot buffalo robe, the horses are shown helping warriors to victory in battle and transporting people and property to new camp sites. In a short time, horses had become crucial to the Plains people's way of life. They could never go back to life on foot.

WILD SPIRIT
An American Indian catches a horse that was roaming wild on the Plains. The new owner would spend weeks teaching the animal to accept a rider on its back. More usually, American Indians would catch horses in raids on other tribes or settlers' camps. Life on the Plains produced a strong and hardy horse.

HORSE RUSTLING
These American Indians appear to be on the lookout. Some tribes bred horses to trade, others were not so honest. The Comanche raiders in Texas would steal horses from other Texans or Mexicans and then trade them to friendly tribes.

OFF OUR LAND

A chief stands on his horse to emphasize the point he is making. The white man is probably marveling at the American Indian's ability to stay upright. Plains Indians were famed for their showmanship and riding skills. The chief's saddle blanket is made from tanned buffalo hide. Most Indian riders used blankets rather than saddles. Tribes, such as the Crow, made bridle ornaments and beaded saddlebags, while others painted symbols on the horses.

TAMING THE HORSE

These boys are attempting to break in a wild horse. When horses were first acquired by tribes, only brave young men and women rode them, although they were used to carry goods. It took about a generation for horses to be accepted.

A TEST OF HONOR

This Blackfoot Indian could be on a horse raid. Stealing horses from another tribe was one way a warrior could prove that he was brave. The raids were not thought of as a crime, more an expression of honor. The Comanche were regarded as the best horsemen and were feared by other tribes and white settlers alike.

COVETED HAIR

Horsehair adorns the head of this Iroquois False Face Mask. American Indians made use of everything around them. Horsehair was used for a variety of things. It could be braided to make rope. It was used as stuffing in a cradle to give a baby some comfortable padding. It could also add the final decoration to an eagle feather headdress.

Markets and Trade

NORTH AMERICAN INDIANS HAD a long tradition of trading. The Hopewell civilizations of about A.D. 200 brought metals and other materials to their centers around the Ohio valley. The Calusas in southern Florida had a vast trade network both inland and across the sea to the Bahamas and Cuba. Many people would travel long distances to buy and sell goods at a regular meeting place. Although some tribes used wampum (shell money), most swapped their goods. People from settled villages exchanged agricultural products such as corn and tobacco for buffalo hides, baskets or eagle feathers from nomadic tribes. When European traders arrived, in the 1600s, they exchanged furs and hides for horses, guns, cotton cloth and metal tools. Early trading posts such as the Hudson's Bay Company were built by whites. These posts were usually on rivers, which could be reached easily by canoe.

BASKETS FOR GOODS
Crafts, such as this Salish basket, were sometimes traded (or swapped) between tribes, and later with Europeans. American Indians particularly wanted wool blankets, while European traders eagerly sought bison robes.

WORDS OF A WAMPUM
A Mohawk chief, King Hendrick of the League of Five Nations, was painted on a visit to Queen Anne's court in London in 1710. He holds a wampum belt made from shells. These were made to record historic events such as the formation of the League of Five Nations of the Iroquois.

COLONIAL TRADERS
A native hunter in Canada offers beaver skins to colonial fur traders in 1777. They would probably have been made into beaver hats. Beaver fur was the most important item the Woodlands tribes had to trade, as competition between European nations for animal skins was fierce. This trade was partly to blame for many tribal conflicts. The Iroquois were renowned beaver hunters who ruthlessly guarded their hunting territory.

SHELL SHOW

A Plains Indian is holding up a wampum belt decorated with shells. The belts were usually associated with the Iroquois and Algonquian tribes who used them to trade, as currency, or to record tribal history. Quahog clam shells were strung together to make a long rectangular belt with patterns showing tribal agreements and treaties. Even colonists used them as currency when there were no coins around.

SAVING SHELLS

Instead of coins, shells or beads made from shells were the main currency. They served as tokens that were swapped for goods. Blue and white shells such as clams and periwinkles were the most prized. These were strung, like beads, on buckskin thongs.

thong   *clam shell*   *mussel shell*

TRADING POSTS

North American Indians would gather in the Hudson's Bay trading post. In return for bringing in pelts (animal furs), the American Indians would be given European goods. Many would be useful, such as iron tools and utensils or colored cloth. Firearms and liquor traded from around 1650 did the tribes more harm than good. As trade increased, more trappers and hunters frequented the trading posts. Later, some of the fur trade posts became military forts and attracted settlers who built towns around them.

Warriors and Warfare

MOST WARS BETWEEN TRIBES were fought over land or hunting territory, and later over horses. As Europeans began to occupy more land, many tribes fought to stop them. Each tribe had warriors, known as braves. There were military societies within the tribe, such as the Cheyenne Dog Soldiers, whose job was to protect the tribe. Warriors would paint both themselves and their horses for spiritual protection. A white stripe across a Blackfoot warrior's face meant vengeance. In the 1700s, Plains tribes traded guns with the Europeans, but they felt that blasting their tribal enemies lacked honor. Instead, warriors developed a way of fighting without killing. A warrior had to get close enough to strike his enemy with a long stick known as a counting coup, then escape unhurt. Each act of bravery earned an honor feather to be tied to the stick.

HEAVY HANDS
Crude tomahawks such as this date back to the Stone Age, but were still used by Plains warriors in the late 1800s. War clubs made from local rocks were vicious weapons, as was the wooden gunstock club, which had a large spike sticking out.

WEAPONS
This tomahawk dates back to around 1750 and once belonged to an Iroquois warrior. Before they acquired firearms, warriors had a variety of weapons of war. They used the bow and arrow, knives, or long lances, as favored by the Comanches from Texas.

HORSEMANSHIP
This Plains warrior displays excellent equestrian skills. He is riding on the side of his horse, holding on with just one foot tucked over the horse's back. This shields him from harm while his hands are free to thrust his spear. Sioux warriors believed that horses fought with their rider in battle. If a warrior died, Apaches would often kill his horse and bury it with its master's body.

MAKE A SHIELD
You will need: *thick cardboard, ruler, pencil, scissors, white glue, glue brush, masking tape, two 14-in. strips of balsa wood dowel ½ in. in diameter, white cotton (or other fabric) approx 16-in. square, red, black and cream or yellow paints, paintbrush, water bowl, brown felt.*

1 Cut two strips of thick cardboard measuring 1 x 46 in. Glue them together to give a double thickness. Then bend them to make a circle.

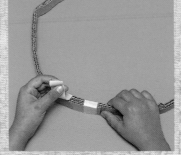

2 Glue and tape the ends together to form a circle, with about 1½ in. overlapping. The diameter should be approximately 14 in. Let dry.

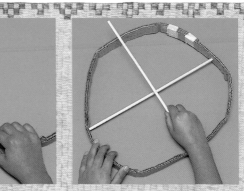

3 Cross and glue the two dowel sticks together at right angles. Glue both to the frame, one from top to bottom, one horizontally. Let the base dry.

WARRIORS' TOOLS

Local hard rock such as obsidian, slate or flint was shaped into knives, arrowheads, spears and axes by striking it with another stone. Bone tools were used to chip away flint to make sharp, fine points. Metal arrowheads were also made from scrap tin from the Europeans.

flint

slate

HERO'S FRIEND

The shield was one of the warrior's most prized possessions. He felt it gave him both spiritual and physical protection. Skin from the bison's neck was used to make it, as this was the toughest part of the animal. It could be decorated with symbols and feathers or scalps.

DRESSED FOR BATTLE

Chief Quanah Parker of the Comanche is wearing his war costume. Each tribe had a war chief who was in charge of planning attacks. He was not usually the leader of the people, but had proved himself to be a brave warrior in battle. Chief Parker led his followers in battles throughout Texas. They fought against the United States in the Red River War of 1874–75. His mother, Cynthia Parker, was a white captive of the tribe.

Warriors often painted animals on their shields. A buffalo head (used here) was a symbol of strength.

4 Lay the fabric flat. Using the frame as a guide, draw around it to make a circle 1 in. wider than the frame. Cut out the circle.

5 Draw a pattern on the fabric, then paint it. A simple, bold pattern works best, or copy our shield and paint a buffalo head. Let the paint dry.

6 Stretch the fabric over the frame, keeping the pattern centered. Glue down the edges all around. Paint the edges red (background color) to neaten them.

7 Cut a strip of brown felt measuring about 1 x 16 in. Glue the ends to the top and bottom edges of the shield at the back. This is the armband.

War and Defeat

From 1775 to 1783, colonists fought for independence from Britain. Some Indians remained neutral in the Revolutionary War, some took sides. At first, the Iroquois League of Nations did not want to be involved in a white man's quarrel. They had, however, allied with the British against the French in other European wars. The League was split and eventually most of the tribes supported the British. In 1777, they ended up fighting some of their own people, the Oneidas, who had sided with the Americans. The United States gained independence in 1783. With new strength, the United States started pushing for more land and introduced the Indian Removal Act of 1830. The aim was to relocate eastern tribes west of the Mississippi River onto reservations (areas set aside for Indians). The Choctaws were the first tribe to be relocated in 1830, to Oklahoma.

Wild West
There were many conflicts between United States soldiers and different tribes, such as this attack in the 1800s. Some attempts at peaceful talks were made. However, military records show that between 1863 and 1891, there were 1,065 fights.

They were followed by the Chickasaws, Creeks and Seminoles. Many long and bitter battles were fought, as the Indians struggled to keep their homelands. Much reservation land was neither as fertile nor as productive as the old tribal land, and some tribes faced starvation.

Trail of Tears
The heartbroken Cherokee nation is being forced to leave its homelands in 1838–39. During the trek west, rain and snow fell, and soldiers made them move on too quickly. It is estimated that almost 4,000 Cherokees died from exhaustion and exposure.

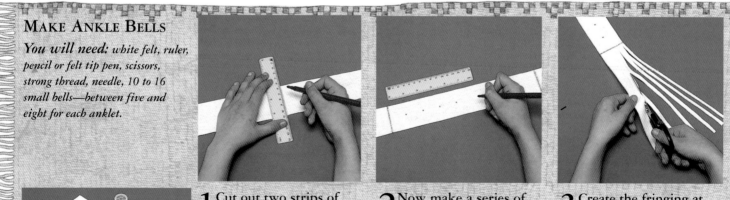

Make Ankle Bells
You will need: white felt, ruler, pencil or felt tip pen, scissors, strong thread, needle, 10 to 16 small bells—between five and eight for each anklet.

1 Cut out two strips of white felt 30 x 2 in. Measure and mark a line across the felt strips, 9½ in. in from one end. Do the same at the other end.

2 Now make a series of marks in the middle section of the strips. Start 1 in. away from one line, then mark every 1 in. This is where the bells will go.

3 Create the fringing at each end of the anklet. Do this by cutting into both ends of the band up to the penciled lines. Do the same for the other anklet.

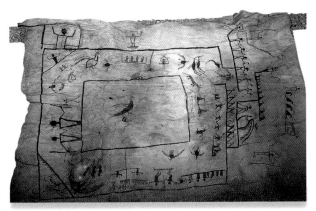

WAR BUNDLE

This buckskin was used to wrap a personal war bundle. It has been painted with the Thunderbird and other supernatural beings for spiritual protection. A bundle might carry a warrior's medicine herbs or warpaint.

THE SHIELD SURVIVED

This warrior's shield belonged to a Dakota (Sioux) warrior in the late 1800s. It may have been used in the Battle of Little Bighorn. The Sioux tribes fought in many battles with the United States around that time. In 1851 their lands were defined by a treaty. Then, when gold was found in Montana, gold hunters broke the treaties by traveling through Sioux land, and war raged again.

THE END OF GENERAL CUSTER

The Battle of Little Bighorn, in 1876, is counted as the last major victory of the North American Indian. Custer's entire 7th Cavalry was defeated by Sioux sub-tribes, after they attacked an Indian village. Sadly, this made United States soldiers even more brutal in their dealings with tribes.

WAR DANCE

Sioux warriors are performing a war dance. During the dance a medicine man would chant and ask for spiritual guidance and protection for warriors going into battle. Other dances were performed after a battle.

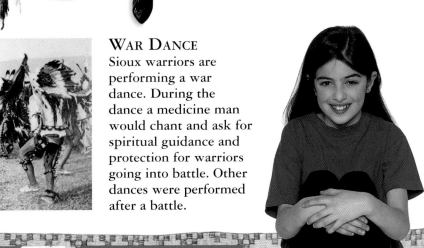

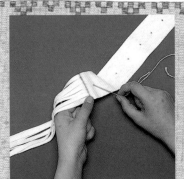

4 Thread a large needle with strong, doubled and knotted thread. Insert the needle into the fabric and pull through until the knot hits the fabric.

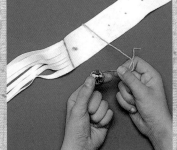

5 Thread the needle through the bell and slip the bell up to the felt. Then insert the needle back into the felt very near the place it came out.

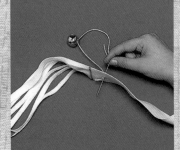

6 Push the needle through and pull tight. Knot the end (opposite side of the bell) to secure and cut away the excess thread. Repeat with the other bells.

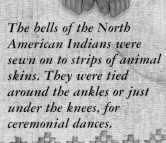

The bells of the North American Indians were sewn on to strips of animal skins. They were tied around the ankles or just under the knees, for ceremonial dances.

Beliefs and Customs

NORTH AMERICAN INDIANS DID NOT believe in a single god. They believed that the changing seasons and events surrounding them were caused by different spirits. To them, everything in the world had a soul or spirit which was very powerful and could help or harm humans. Spirits had to be treated with respect, so prayers, songs, chants and dances would be offered to please them. The most important spirit to the Sioux was Wakan Tanka, the Great Spirit or Great Mysterious, who was in charge of all other spirits. The Navajo believed in the Holy People. These were Sky, Earth, Moon, Sun, Hero Twins, Thunders, Winds and Changing Woman. Some tribes believed in ghosts. Western Shoshonis, Salish (Flathead) people and Ojibwas considered ghosts to be spirit helpers who acted as bodyguards in battle. The leader of ceremonies was the shaman (medicine man) who conducted the dances and rites. He also acted as a doctor. The shamans of California would treat a sick person by sucking out the pain, spitting it out and sending it away.

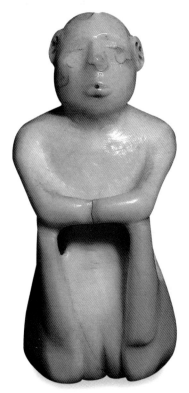

CHARMED LIFE
A whale's tusk was used to carve this Inuit shaman's charm. Spirits called tuneraks were thought to help the angakok, as the Inuit shaman was called, in his duties. The role of shaman was passed from father to son. In Padlimuit, Copper and Iglulik tribes, women could also be shamans.

BEAR NECESSITIES OF LIFE
This shaman is nicknamed Bear's Belly and belonged to the Arikara Plains tribe. Shamans were powerful, providing the link between humans and spirits. After years of training, they could cure ailments, tell the future or speak to the dead.

MAKE A RATTLE
You will need: thick cardboard, pencil, ruler, scissors, masking tape, compass, white glue, brush, two balsa wood strips 1 in. wide and about 7 in. long, raffia or string, air-drying clay, wooden skewer, cream, black, orange/red and brown paint, paintbrushes, water bowl, black thread, needle.

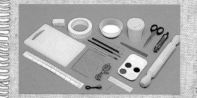

1 Cut two pieces of cardboard ½ in. wide, one 18 in. long and one 23 in. long. Cover both in masking tape. Make holes about 1 in. apart along the strips.

2 Bend each strip into a ring. Glue and tape the ends together to make two rings. Glue the two strips of balsa wood into a cross to fit across the large ring.

3 Glue the two sticks together, then strap them with raffia or string. Wrap the string around one side, then cross it over the center. Repeat on all sides.

NATURAL REMEDY

Medicine men used a variety of potions to cure ailments. These included herbs and plants such as nettles, yarrow, willow, jimson-weed and tobacco or red ants. They might be fed to the sick patient, put on the skin or waved around them to ward off evil.

thoroughwort

yarrow

skunk cabbage

willow bark

THE HAPPY COUPLE

Menominee people of the Woodlands made these dolls to celebrate the marriage of a couple. The miniature man and woman were tied face to face to keep husband and wife faithful. Dolls feature in the customs of many tribes, especially the Hopi and Zuni of the Southwest. Their kachina dolls are spirits shown in the form of animals, humans or plants.

MEDICINE BAGS

Crystals, animal parts, feathers and powders made of ground up plants and vegetables might be inside these bundles. They were used to make cures and spells by a shaman (medicine man) of the Winnebago tribe from the Woodlands.

Rattles were an important part of any ceremony. In some tribes only shamans could hold one.

SACRED BIRD

Rattles, such as this Thunderbird rattle from the Northwest Coast, were considered sacred objects and carved with the images of spirits. They were made of animal hoofs, rawhide or turtle shells, and filled with seeds or pebbles. Some were hand held, others were put on necklaces.

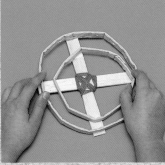

4 Glue the two cardboard rings onto the cross, as here. The larger ring sits on the outer ends of the cross. The smaller one is roughly ½–1 in. inside of that.

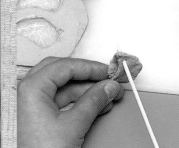

5 Roll out the clay to a ½-in. thickness. Cut out 20 to 30 semicircle shapes to resemble penguin beaks. Use a stick to make a hole at one end.

6 When the beaks are dry, paint them cream. Let dry. Paint the tips black, then paint red or orange stripes. Next, paint the two rings brown.

7 Thread the black cotton through the hole in a painted beak, then tie it through one of the holes in the rings. Repeat with each beak, filling both rings.

The Sweat Lodge and Other Rites

STEAM AND SMOKE
A holy man, such as this Pima shaman, would be in charge of sweats. Prayers and chants were offered, and the sacred pipe was passed around each time the door was opened.

SWEATING PURIFIED THE BODY and mind according to North American Indians. The Sioux called it "fire without end." The sweat ritual was one of the most important and ancient of all North American religious rituals. They were among the first people to use heat to cleanse the body. But for tribe members, it was not simply a question of hygiene. The sweat lodge rite was performed before and after other ceremonies to symbolize moving in and out of a sacred world. Warriors prepared their spirits before the Sun Dance ceremony by taking a sweat bath. This was a dance to give thanks for food and gifts received during the year, and often featured self-mutilation. Sweats were also taken to purify the body and as a medical treatment to cure illness. They were often one of various customs, such as rites of passage from childhood to adulthood. A young boy who was about to make his transition into warrior-life was invited to spend time with the tribe's males. They would offer him the sacred pipe, which was usually smoked to send prayers. This was called Hunka's ceremony and showed the tribe's acceptance that the boy was ready. Some warrior initiation rites were brutal—such as the Mandan's custom of suspending young men by wooden hooks pierced through their chest, or scarring them, known as Okipa. Both girls and boys prepared for passing into adolescence by spending time alone and fasting (not eating).

BUILDING A SWEAT LODGE
These two American Indian girls stand beside their family sweat lodge. Two main types of lodges were used, the earth-covered lodge or this variety, built of saplings then covered with blankets, canvas or hide. The blankets would be removed between sweats. The stones were heated outside then carried in. Steam was created by pouring water over the stones.

BATHS IN EARTH

An American Indian crawls out from an earth-covered sweat lodge for air. Six to eight people could sit around the hot stones inside, depending on the size of the sweat lodge. Males and females would both take part in sweats, but it was customary to do so separately. In some tribes, families built their own family lodges, and some larger sweat lodges were also used as homes or temples. Sticks and wood formed the frame. This was covered in mud or clay. The fire would be built in the lodge, causing a dry heat. It was dark, stuffy and hot, similar to the saunas used in Europe. However, a sweat lodge was used to cleanse the spirit as well as the skin.

CLEANSED AND REFRESHED

Herbs, such as sweetgrass and cedar, were often put on the hot stones inside a sweat lodge. When the water was poured over the stones, the smell and essence of the herbs were released into the lodge with the steam. Herbs helped to clear the nasal passages. They could also be selected to treat particular ailments. As the heat from the steam opened up the skin's pores, the herbs could enter the body and work at the illness or help purify the spirit. Sweating removed toxins (poisons in the body) and, the American Indians believed, forced out disease.

GROWING UP

A young Apache girl is dressed up for a modern tribal ceremony. The lives of North American Indians were filled with rituals to mark each milestone in a person's life or important tribal events. There were ceremonies for birth, for becoming an adult and to mark changing seasons.

INSTRUMENTS TELL A STORY

This Tsimshian rattle has been involved in many ceremonies. Tribes had a vast amount of ceremonial objects, from rattles to headdresses, clothing and wands. Their decorations were usually of spiritual significance. In some tribes, the frog was respected, since it would croak when danger was near. Others believed that their long tongues could suck out evil. A frog also stars in creation myths of the Nez Perce.

Sacred Dances

Dancing was an important part of North American Indian life. Some of the sacred dances were performed before or after great events such as births, deaths, marriages, hunts or battle, but they meant more than a big party. The Green Corn Dance was held annually to start the Creek New Year and celebrate agricultural growth. The Arikara Bear Dance hoped to influence the growth of corn and squash crops. Dancers often wore costumes. The Cheyenne Sun dancers painted their upper body black (for clouds) with white dots (for hail). The Assiniboine Clown dancers often danced and talked backward and wore masks with long noses.

DOG DANCE
A Hidatsa warrior from the Crazy Dog Soldier Society performs the Dog Dance to thank spirits for his strength. His headdress is made from magpie tail feathers with a crest of turkey tail feathers. The Hidatsa on the Missouri had many societies, including the White Buffalo Society, a women's group. The White Buffalo Woman was a mythical spirit.

SNOWSHOE DANCE
The Snowshoe Dance was performed after the first snow each winter by some Woodlands tribes. To the Indians, snow meant the passing of a year. People would speak of something happening two snows ago. Winter was a hard time, food was scarce with few animals around to hunt. The dance asked spirits for help to survive.

MAKE A DANCE WAND
You will need: white paper, ruler, pencil, scissors, black and cream paint, paintbrush, water pot, 8 8-in. lengths of balsa stick 3mm thick, white glue, glue brush, compasses, thick cardboard, red and orange paper, a stick 30 in. long and ½ in. thick, string.

1 Cut out eight feather shapes 8 in. long from white paper. Make cuts on the top edges and paint the tips black. Glue sticks 1½ in. from the top of the feather.

2 Use a compass to measure out two semicircles with a diameter of 2 in. on the cardboard. Cut out both semicircles. Hold the feathers by the sticks.

3 Glue the bottom end of the feathers between the two cardboard semicircles. Arrange them around the curved edge. Leave the straight edge unstuck.

PREPARING FOR WAR

Only men joined in war dances such as this Sioux ceremony. Warriors were preparing themselves for conflict. They hoped to gain favor with the spirits who would protect them from their enemies. Deer tails and feathers might hang on dance wands, but lances and spears had more grisly decorations. They displayed trophies of war such as the head of the enemy or scalps (a patch of skin and hair cut from an enemy in battle).

NATIVE KILT

This buckskin apron (or kilt) was once worn by a shaman during ceremonial dances. It is decorated with a picture of a beaver, a native North American animal. The beaver is this shaman's totem, a spirit helper. The spirit would be called upon to give the dancer strength to drive away sickness and evil spirits, and bring luck.

Ceremonial wands were carried during dances. Sometimes just one huge eagle feather or an animal tail hung from the top.

4 Draw and cut out 12 2½-in. long feathers from the red and orange paper. Make eight more red ones, 1 in. long. Make feathery cuts into the top edges.

5 Divide the 2½-in. feathers in half and glue them to each end of the long stick. Secure them with string tied around the stick and bottom of feathers.

6 Paint the semicircles cream, then dry. Bend back the two straight edges. Place the flaps on either side of the center of the stick. Glue them firmly in place.

7 Glue the smaller red feathers to the outside tips of the black feathers (one on each). Let dry. Your wand is ready, so let the dance begin.

Death and Burial

A DEATH IN THE TRIBE was followed by a solemn ceremony. North American Indians believed in spirits and often an afterlife, so the dead person had to be properly prepared for it. The Pueblo Indians would rub cornmeal on the body and place a cotton mask over the face. Cheyenne mourners would dress the dead in a pair of moccasins with beaded soles. This meant they could walk on the clouds to meet their relatives in the Always Summer Land (afterworld). Apaches would kill a warrior's horse to accompany its master. Bodies would be buried or burned depending on custom. The early Hohokam cremated their dead and placed the ashes in pots and these were buried. Some tribes, Crees of the Plains for example, buried their dead in the ground, while other clans, such as the Mandan, placed bodies under earth mounds. Stone graves, or the dead person's home were also used. The Apaches took their dead far away and placed the bodies in mountain crevices. Both the Apaches and the Navajo were very superstitious and afraid of ghosts. They burned the dead person's house and burned or broke the contents to stop the ghost from coming back to earth. Some Pueblo people smashed painted pottery and buried it with the dead body to symbolize the release of the soul.

FUNERARY DOLL
Funerary effigies, such as this doll from California, were used during the funeral ceremony and buried with the body. Some tribes had annual food offerings to keep the ghosts happy.

MORTUARY POLE
Haida people placed human remains in grave boxes. These were put on top of a short totem pole called a mortuary pole, usually carved from a red cedar tree. A potlatch ceremony (a feast where gifts were given) would be held. This material display would show that the dead person had been valued.

PROTECTED IN DEATH
This is a wooden gravemarker from the Northwest Coast. It was carved using stone tools. Many tribes carved figures for their dead. The Zuni carved effigies of the War Gods (guardians of the people) from wood that had been struck by lightning. These would be placed at the entrance of a tomb to protect it. Other figures and effigies were left to keep the dead person company.

HAIDA HEAD
A member of a Haida family is remembered in this carving. Many totem (spirit) figures were of tribal ancestors, as a way of keeping the dead person's memory alive. Other carvings of mythical figures have been found on totem and mortuary poles.

REMEMBERING THE DEAD
The death of an important tribe member has been recorded on this painted buckskin from the Kiowa and Comanche tribe. Most of the Plains tribes used the burial platform, which was usually placed in trees. The Huron people of the Woodlands also placed their dead on a platform. Later, the rotted body was carried to a cemetery, where the remains were placed in a small cabin (spirit house). The mourners put food, oil, tools and presents inside to assist the spirit in the afterworld.

SOUL FOOD
Just as food was a driving factor in tribal life, so it was in death. Many tribes left food as offerings for dead relatives. The Shawnee Feast of the Dead was held each year to honor the spirits of dead tribal members. They would place sumptuous fruits and food on the graves and light candles all around.

plums

artichoke

HOUSE OF SPIRITS
Bright grave markers rest on an Inuit spirit house in Alaska. The Inuit believed that the souls of humans (and animals) came back into the world again as someone else. Animals could become human. When people or animals died, tribe members celebrated their spirit, including animals they had hunted.

BURIAL PLATFORM
The tall stick scaffolding in this picture is a burial platform. Bodies of the dead were placed high off the ground to prevent wolves or coyotes from eating them. They would stay there, wrapped with cloth or a buffalo robe, until the skin had rotted. The remains would be buried.

North American Indians Today

MODERN CEREMONIES
This couple is joining other American Indian descendants at a powwow (tribal gathering). The meetings are popular because of a recent surge of interest in the culture of the tribes. Powwows give the people a chance to dress in traditional costume, speak their native language and learn more about their tribal history.

R ECORDS SHOW THAT BY 1900 the American Indian population north of Mexico was down from between 2.5 and 3 million, to 400,000. Today the figure is in the region of 1,750,000. From the 1800s, many North American Indians were moved by the United States government from their homelands to areas of land known as reservations. In Canada, the lands are called reserves. There are several hundred of these, smaller in size than the United States reservations, but the American Indians were not moved. About 300 United States federal reservations still exist today, some for a single tribe, others as home to a number of groups. In the 1900s, American Indians became more politically active, helped by political groups such as the American Indian Movement (AIM). Tribes began seeking compensation for lost land. The Cherokees were awarded 15 million dollars for lands they had lost. Many reservations are now governed by the tribes. Some are run by a council with an elected chief. In a way, it is similar to traditional tribal society. However, the United States government still has control over much surviving American Indian land. Since 1970, tribes have been allowed to run their reservation schools and to teach children their ancestral history.

TRIBAL PROTEST
In July of 1978 these American Indians walked for five months to Washington from their reservations to protest to Congress. At protest meetings, leaders read from a list of 400 treaties, all the promises that the United States had broken. For years, many tribes tried to get back land taken from them. In 1992, Navajo and Hopi tribes were given back 1.8 million acres of their land in Northern Arizona to be divided between the tribes.

SODA FOUNTAIN STOP
A Seminole family enjoys sodas in 1948 in a Miami store. Tribes gradually adapted to the American ways of life, but some kept their own customs and dress. Seminoles were forced from Florida to Oklahoma in 1878. Almost 300 refused to leave the Everglades, and about 2,000 live there today.

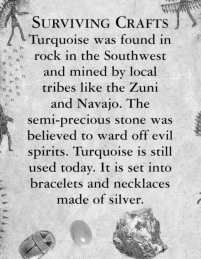

SURVIVING CRAFTS

Turquoise was found in rock in the Southwest and mined by local tribes like the Zuni and Navajo. The semi-precious stone was believed to ward off evil spirits. Turquoise is still used today. It is set into bracelets and necklaces made of silver.

turquoise   *silver*

THE TOURIST TRAIL

A traditional Inuit scene of snowshoes propped outside an igloo. Most people in Alaska and Greenland live in modern, centrally heated homes. However, the ancient skills of building temporary shelters from ice bricks still survive. They are passed down to each generation and occasionally used by hunters or tourists eager to experience North American Indian customs.

CHEERLEADING CHIEF

Dressed in full ceremonial costume, this North American Indian helps conduct celebrations at a football stadium. It is a way of raising awareness of the existence of tribes. The cheerleading is not far removed from a war chief's tribal role of encouraging warriors in battle.

STITCHING THE PAST

Traditional American Indian crafts are still made today. The method of curing hides has remained the same. No chemicals are used during the tanning process, and the scraping is still done by hand. However, styles of crafts had already changed to suit the European market in the 1600s when traders brought in new materials.

TRADITIONAL SKILLS

An Indian craftsman produces beautiful jewelry in silver and turquoise. Zuni and Navajo people were among the finest jewelry makers in this style. Other tribes, such as the Crow, are famous for their beadwork.

Glossary

A

adobe Plaster used by Pueblo Indians on their homes. It was made from clay and straw.

Algonquian A group of many tribes (including the Secotan and Powhatan) who shared the same coastal areas in the northeast and spoke a version of the same language.

ancestor A family member who died long ago.

angakok A name for an Inuit shaman (medicine man).

archaeologist Person who studies ancient remains or ruins.

B

bark Outer layer (covering) of tree trunks.

blubber Fat of a whale, found just beneath the skin.

C

caribou Reindeer found in North America.

cavalry Soldiers on horseback.

clan A group of people who are related to each other.

colonies Communities or groups of people who settle in another land, but still keep links with their own country.

Congress Legislative branch of the United States government.

cradleboard A wooden board, usually with protective head area, to which a baby was strapped and carried around.

currency Form of exchange for goods such as money or wampum.

D

descendant Person who is descended from (born after) an individual or group of people who lived earlier.

dialects Regional accents and language variations.

dugout canoe A canoe made by hollowing out a tree trunk.

E

effigy Figure or doll representing someone.

F

frontiers Land on the border between Indian territory and land European settlers had already taken or bought.

G

glyphs Pictures that tell a message or have a meaning.

H

hunter-gatherer Person who lives by hunting animals and gathering wild roots and plants.

I

ice floes Large sheets of ice floating in the sea.

immigrants People who come to live in a land from other countries.

Inuit The native people of the North American Arctic, Canada and Greenland as distinguished from Asia and the Aleutian islands. Inuit is also the general name for an Eskimo in Canada.

Iroquois A group of tribes from the Woodlands who joined together to form a powerful government.

K

kiva Underground chamber used for religious ceremonies among Pueblo people.

Kwatee Mythical figure connected with tales of the creation of the universe.

L

lacrosse Stick and ball game played with a stick with a net on the end. The ball is scooped in the net rather than hit in the air or along the ground.

legend Ancient story that has been handed down over the years. It may be part myth and part truth.

legislation Making laws.

loom A frame used for weaving yarn into fabric and blankets.

M

migrating When a group of people, animals or birds travel between different habitats to settle in other regions either permanently or at specific times of the year.

missionaries Religious people who went to North America to change the North American Indians' religion from their own traditional beliefs to Christianity, which was the prominent religion in Europe.

moccasins Soft leather, slip-on shoes often decorated with beads.

myth An old tale or legend that describes gods, spirits or fantastic creatures.

N

nation Group of people who live in one territory and usually share the same language or history.

nomadic People who move from one area to another to find food, better land or to follow herds.

O

obsidian Dark, glassy volcanic rock found in the earth.

Oglala Sioux A band of the Western or Teton Sioux.

P

parka Hooded, warm overcoat usually made of caribou or other animal skin and worn by Inuit people in the Arctic.

pelts Skin or fur of a furry animal such as a beaver.

pemmican Food mixture made from ground bison meat, berries and animal fat.

pictographs Picture writing.

Pueblo People from the Southwest who lived in villages built of mud and stone.

Q

quahog Edible round clam found in North America.

R

reservation An area of land chosen by the United States government and set aside for a tribe(s) in the 1800s. Sometimes early reservation land was seized again later by the US and tribes were moved on again to another reservation further away.

rites Solemn procedure normally carried out for a religious purpose or part of a ceremony.

rituals An often repeated set of actions carried out during a religious or other ceremony.

S

sauna Bath of hot steam.

scalps Chunks of skin and long hair which warriors shaved off the heads of their enemy in battle.

settlers People who came from other countries to settle or stay in North America.

shaman The medicine man or woman of the tribe. These people were spiritual and ceremonial leaders and doctors.

shrine A holy place used for worship, often built beside graves.

T

tepee Conical tent with a frame of poles, covered with animal skins, used by Plains Indians.

tomahawk War ax. Its head was of stone, metal or bone.

totem A good luck charm.

totem pole A tall post carved with totems.

trading post General store where people from a wide area traded or swapped goods.

tradition Habits, beliefs or practices handed down from one generation to the next.

trappers People who trap animals, especially for their skin.

travois A V-shaped frame for carrying possessions dragged by dogs and later by horses.

treaty Peace agreement.

tribe Group of people who shared a common language and way of life.

W

wigwam Dwelling made of bark, rushes or skins spread over arched poles lashed together.

wampum Shells, or beads made from shells, strung together and used as currency or to record a historical event.

Index